PRAISE FOR
IN FULL FLOOD

'Finbarr Flood writes in straightforward but touching terms of the poverty of the times . . . His insights into the industrial-relations dilemmas of the 1990s are fascinating'

SUNDAY INDEPENDENT

'A thoroughly enjoyable read'

George Hook, THE RIGHT HOOK

'[*In Full Flood* is] not only an engrossing account of a fascinating and eventful life, it is also a valuable insight into the evolution of the Irish economy from a static and tradition-laden monolith into the dynamic Celtic Tiger economy that now sees Ireland ranked amongst the wealthiest countries in the world.'

IRISH BOOK REVIEW

First published in 2006 by Liberties Press
Liberties Press | 51 Stephens Road | Inchicore | Dublin 8 | Ireland
www.libertiespress.com | info@libertiespress.com
Editorial: +353 (1) 402 0805 | sean@libertiespress.com
Sales and marketing: +353 (1) 453 4363 | peter@libertiespress.com
Liberties Press is a member of Clé, the Irish Book Publishers' Association

Trade enquiries to CMD Distribution
55A Spruce Avenue | Stillorgan Industrial Park | Blackrock | County Dublin
Tel: +353 (1) 294 2560
Fax: +353 (1) 294 2564

Sales representation by Compass Ireland Independent Book Sales
38 Kerdiff Avenue | Naas | County Kildare
Tel: +353 (45) 880 805
Fax: +353 (45) 880 806

Copyright © Finbarr Flood, 2006

ISBN 1–905483–02–3

2 4 6 8 10 9 7 5 3

A CIP record for this title is available from the British Library

Cover design by Liam Furlong at space.ie
Set in 11.5-point Garamond

Printed in Ireland by Colour Books
Unit 105 | Baldoyle Industrial Estate | Dublin 13

# IN FULL FLOOD

## FINBARR FLOOD

LIBERTIES

# CONTENTS

To Anne

for taking such great care of me in recent times and
for loving me and bringing peace and calmness into my life

# ACKNOWLEDGEMENTS

Without Catherine McGoldrick, there would be no book. With her usual good nature, which I relied upon so heavily when she was my assistant in Personnel and later when I was managing director of Guinness, she typed, retyped and changed my text. With her usual tact and diplomacy, she suggested many of the changes, improvements and ways of avoiding being sued for libel over the eighteen months this tome has been in the melting pot. Thank you, Catherine.

Thank you to Barbara Richie for typing the first few chapters and encouraging me to continue with it. To my parents Jack and Eva, for all the memories. To my sisters Kalleen and Mary (Hanley), Mary's husband Bernie, their sons John and Colm, their daughter Eimear and husband Brendan, and their son Brian and fiancée Shirley, for their continued support and friendship. To my son Barry, of whom I am extremely proud: the fact that he has written a number of very important books in his field gave me the impetus to start this one. To my daughter Suzie, who has given us all two treasured little boys, Josh and Alex – who have both given us so much happiness. To my wife Anne, who as yet has not read the book: thank you for putting up with the papers all over the house, the long quiet hours as I buried myself away and the copious cups of tea. To my dear Aunt Cathy, who died in 2002, and who gave me a great start in life and an interest in sport, especially football, spending most of her years looking out for me like a second mother. To the many friends who have read the drafts and given such useful feedback and suggestions. To Liberties Press, who have taken the publishing of this book on board and who have done a great job with it. Finally, a big thank you to Mr Russell, ENT Consultant at Our Lady's Hospital for Sick Children Crumlin, together with his team; all the other specialists and their teams; the staff of the hospital, particularly Nazareth Ward, for all the expertise and care they have given to Alex, who spent seventeen months as an inpatient in the hospital. I am donating the author royalties of this book to furthering the good work being done for children who need tracheostomies under the auspices of Mr Russell.

# INTRODUCTION

Over the years, many people have said to me that I should write a book in relation to my experiences in business and in sport, and particularly about the Guinness I joined as a boy of fourteen. This is probably because I pontificated so often about what life was like growing up in Dublin in the fifties.

I never envisaged writing a book, but when I retired from the Labour Court I sat down and, for some unknown reason, started to have a go at writing. Initially, I took to it like duck to water. It seemed simple to repeat the stories that I had bored people to death with over many years.

As I progressed, I enjoyed reliving various aspects of my life. I now believe that everybody should put down on paper their memories – the good and the bad things that happened to them – and to leave behind a record of their feelings at various stages of their lives.

One of the things I found most difficult in writing the book was trying to get on paper the flavour of incidents or stories. Many of them were nowhere near as interesting or funny in print as they were when they were told aloud.

So why have I written the book? For a number of reasons. My wife says it's an ego trip. I believe that, having started it, I had to prove that I could do it. For a guy with little formal education, no self-confidence, and a massive inferiority complex growing up, I've been extremely lucky, managing to hold down three of the best jobs in the country, across the private, public and sporting sectors.

Becoming managing director of the most famous brewery in the world, one that had been in existence for more than two hundred years, was a hell of a thrill, particularly given the climate of class distinction that prevailed in Guinness in 1953 when I joined.

After working for forty-one years for Guinness, my luck held out again when I was offered the deputy chairmanship of the Labour Court, with the promise of becoming chairman. Even the title has a ring of authority to it. Knowing the esteem in which the Court is held nationally and the role it has played, not only in the business world but also in the affairs of the country, it was a great honour to be asked to do the job.

The third success I enjoyed was being appointed chairman of of Shelbourne Football Club, the club which I had played for as a young professional. Not many people are lucky enough to achieve this, and I was extremely grateful to the Donnelly family when they asked me to take over as chairman.

In all three jobs, luck played a part: luck that Joe Costello fiddled my weight to get into Guinness, luck that I was retiring from Guinness as the deputy chairman job at the Labour Court became available, and luck that I was back in football to become chairman of Shelbourne.

In writing the book, I want to give encouragement to young people who at various stages of their lives may meet difficult situations, or may have to work in mundane or soul-destroying occupations. In the Brewery, I worked in some of the worst jobs imaginable over the years. They were completely monotonous and offered no job satisfaction. I hope that when young people in these type of jobs read the story of my fifty years of work, they will believe that the opportunities will come. I hope too that they are encouraged to fulfil their potential and that, when life is difficult, they remember the ups and downs that most people encounter before they are successful.

Another group that I hope will enjoy the book is the people I worked with over the years in the Brewery. The book is written to commemorate all those who went into the Brewery with few prospects of anything other than labouring work, who were taken out of school before their full potential was identified, and who, with a bit of luck – or in another company – could have been extremely successful. The book is also to thank all those people who have guided and looked after me over the years, whether when I was a child playing football for schoolboy clubs or in the Brewery. Over the years, many people have told me that they carried me during my working days because I was a lazy so-and-so and was always wanting to thwart the system. To them I say thank you, and hope that they get some satisfaction from seeing that I didn't waste their efforts.

The Brewery was for many a way of life, a unique culture, and I hope that the hundreds of people that I worked with there will relate to the picture I paint of the Guinness that we grew up in. I hope their families, who lived the Brewery way of life, will also enjoy the stories of the years gone by, particularly now that Guinness as a company no longer exists.

I hope that those who, like myself, grew up in the fifties and sixties, an era of great innocence, and whose lives were dominated by football and the dance halls, will get some enjoyment from the book and that my reminiscences will give them some pleasure and record for posterity what life was like then.

Finally, probably the principal reason why I persevered in writing the book was for my two grandchildren, Josh, who has given Anne and me such tremendous pleasure in his eight years, and Alex, who in two and a half years has made his presence felt in many ways. The book will give both of them a picture of what their grandfather was like. One of my big worries over the last few years, since I had major surgery in 2002 for an aneurysm, is that I might not live long enough for the two boys to remember me. I now feel that the pressure is off – that even if they don't remember me (although I think Josh is at the age that he will), they can read about their grandfather and maybe get a feel for what he was like.

I hope that everyone who reads the book gets as much satisfaction and pleasure out of it as I have had in writing it. Despite the trials and tribulations, and the hours spent getting it all down, I have enjoyed going down memory lane and reliving the rare aul' times.

# 1

## GROWING UP IN COWTOWN

My childhood years were spent growing up in the forties and fifties around the Oxmantown Road area in Dublin 7, affectionately known as Cowtown. This area, covering Oxmantown Road, Manor Street, Aughrim Street and all the surrounding roads, was nicknamed Cowtown because the cattle market was situated beside Aughrim Street Church. This market spanned an area from Aughrim Street across to Prussia Street and up to the North Circular Road. It was held every Wednesday from four o'clock in the morning until some time in the early afternoon.

On Tuesday night, hundreds of cattle, sheep and pigs would arrive in the area and be held in the side streets, ready for the opening of the market on Wednesday morning. It was extremely difficult to sleep, with hundreds of animals moving about in the confined spaces of the road outside – just like the Wild West. When we came out in the morning, we often skated down the street on the cow dung that had accumulated on the road and footpath overnight.

A lot of trade was done in the market each week. As children, we benefited: we were allowed to milk the cows and take the milk home, and we were hired by the drovers to help drive the cattle down the North Circular Road towards the North Wall, for despatch by CIÉ railway wagons all over the country.

We would run ahead of the cattle, brandishing our 'cattle sticks', made from branches taken from the trees in the Phoenix Park, and block off the side streets, preventing any of the cattle from deviating from the straight line to the North Wall. Unfortunately, a cow would sometimes go mad and run amok, rampaging through a shop and wrecking everything in its path. The general panic and damage to shops and property added to the excitement of living in the area for us children. On arrival at the North Wall, we were usually paid a penny or two for our efforts. We would then walk back home, very pleased with ourselves, as we were able to buy enough sweets to sicken ourselves.

Our family – my father Jack, my mother Eva, my sisters Kalleen and Mary, and myself – lived in the artisan dwelling cottages and houses from the early forties to the early sixties. We had earlier lived on the High Road in Kilmainham and on Errigal Road in Drimnagh for very brief spells.

The Artisan Dwellings Company owned and managed cottages and houses in the Harold's Cross and Oxmantown Road areas of Dublin. The system they operated could be of considerable benefit today in addressing the problems facing first-time buyers. Rented two-bedroom cottages were given on a priority basis to young couples with one or two children, with the two-bedroom, two-storey houses going to bigger families with children of both sexes, and the three-bedroom houses going to the biggest families.

Within the company, a system operated that allowed tenants to swap houses or to make a request to the company to be put on a list to be transferred to a bigger house. Correspondingly, parents who had raised their families and were now living alone would often look for a smaller house, and move back to a two-bedroom house or even a cottage.

The flexibility afforded by this system, and the method of swapping, was a tremendous way of dealing with the problems that people encountered as their families grew or, alternatively, as they got older and their accommodation requirements changed. The practice prevailed right up to the 1960s, at which stage the Artisan Dwellings Company decided to get out of the property business and sold off the houses to the residents at a reasonable rate. Many of the residents in turn sold the houses at a profit and moved out of the area. Indeed, my father and mother took advantage of this arrangement and moved to Tallaght in 1963 – a move my father later regretted, as he missed being able to walk everywhere, particularly into town.

While the procedure for swapping required a formal application to the company, an informal barter system also operated: very often, money changed hands between tenants in order to encourage people to agree to a swap. An additional attraction, or bartering lever, existed if the cottage or house had been renovated, with the addition of a bathroom or an extension. These amenities would increase the chances of getting somebody with a bigger house to swap and trade down. The clincher was often money, quietly passed between tenants: even then, the brown envelope was king!

In our case, we were originally offered a cottage on Infirmary Road, but my parents were not happy with the state it was in and gave back the key. We were very lucky that we subsequently got the key of a cottage in Ross Street, just off Oxmantown Road. The cottage had two bedrooms, a small kitchen and a dining room. We lived there for a number of years before obtaining a swap with people on Oxmantown Road for a two-bedroom, two-storey house.

The advantage of this swap was that, while there were only two bedrooms, the downstairs parlour, as it was called, could be used as a third bedroom, with me sleeping on a bed settee. While this gave the family an additional bedroom, the downside was that, as I was the person who slept in it, I had to stay up until any visitors had gone, because they were sitting on my bed!

Eventually, we did another swap with the Mahony family, whose son was a schoolteacher in St Gabriel's School, off Aughrim Street, and we went to live on the corner of Kirwan

Street and Manor Street. We moved to a *three*-bedroom house, with a sitting room, parlour and bathroom, looking up Manor Place and down Manor Street. We had arrived! Manor Street had some houses and shops on it, but it was primarily pubs. In fact, it had more pubs in it than any other street of its size anywhere in Ireland.

When we first moved from Drimnagh into Ross Street, a street of around thirty cottages, my father built on an extension to the house. Unfortunately, from the day it was built, the extension leaked. We spent a lot of time dashing about the place with buckets and basins, trying to collect all the water that came through the roof when it rained. Most importantly, though, an extension improved the chances of a swap to a bigger house.

There was a tremendous community spirit in the area, with people always there to help and support each other in time of need, sharing the successes and disappointments of life. People took pride in success achieved by anyone in the area. Nowadays, neighbours frequently don't seem to know the person living next door – and, what's more, don't *want* to know them.

At the bottom of Ross Street was Reddy's sweet shop, which sold Peggy's legs, bull's eyes, liquorice pipes and lucky bags. Opposite was H. Williams; the big attraction there was broken biscuits for a penny. If you were lucky, the jar could be full of custard creams or other delicious biscuits; on the other hand, you could be stuck with a bag of broken Marietta biscuits!

I kept about a dozen pigeons in a loft in our small yard at the back of the cottage in Ross Street. Most of my time was spent trying to prevent my pals the Eleberts, who lived two doors away, from seducing my best pigeons into their loft. Once the pigeons went there, they wouldn't come back, as it was their nature to settle in. I had to keep the pigeons well fed to hold on to them.

No one on our street, or in the vicinity, had a car until one day a car appeared outside No. 10, the Agers. My recollection is that it was a black Ford Prefect. It was parked outside all week, and the family went driving in it on a Sunday. We kids were allowed to sit in it on a number of occasions, out of the rain. We were mesmerised by the sound of the rain beating down on the roof as we all sat there in silence. To this day, the sound of rain beating down holds a great fascination for me.

As children, we spent all our time playing in Ross Street. Certainly in the early years, we never ventured much further. It was an era of self-entertainment: there were no PlayStations or PCs. Most children were put out on the street to play early in the morning and stayed there until late at night, only being allowed in for their meals. The day was spent playing 'king' or 'penny in the hole', banging a ball off the gable end of a cottage, or playing cricket by bowling from one side of the road to a tar wicket on the gable end of a house. The tarred wicket is still there to this day.

Some years ago, when I was interviewed for Patrick O'Dea's book *A Class of their Own,* about people growing up in Ireland and whether they were affected by class distinction or snobbery, I was asked by the author where we played as children. When he asked me what other streets we played in, it suddenly dawned on me that we never strayed away from our own patch. I knew immediately that the next question was going to cause me problems: when he asked me why, I had to give him the simple answer that our mothers wouldn't let us. At the time, I remember thinking that this sounded extraordinary, given that children nowadays seem to have the freedom to do practically anything they want. In those days, if you were told not to do something, you just didn't do it.

Years later, when my own children, Barry and Suzie, were growing up, I tried to impose the same discipline by saying 'Don't do that', but I was immediately confronted by the query 'Why not?' On many occasions, not having an answer, I flipped my hand and said 'Because I'm your father.' Needless to say, this didn't work. We have now moved on into an era when many children are allowed to run free and do as they like – or, to use the politically correct explanation, to 'express themselves'. We have entered the age of 'free-range children'.

In the small street where we lived, there were three major personalities: Kevin Matthews, the Dublin hurling goalkeeper; Frank Radford, who captained the Transport football team and later played for Shamrock Rovers; and Noel Fitzsimons, a cricketer who played for Phoenix and also for Ireland. Not bad for such a small street!

Kevin Matthews' mother was a frail woman who was confined to bed a lot of the time. I ran errands for her most days. She usually got twenty cigarettes and the *Evening Herald;* I was paid weekly for my troubles. She also liked a flutter on the horses. I would go down to the bookies in the Lucky Lane, just off Oxmantown Road, to place the bets. I queued outside the shop to get one of the older men to put the bet on for me and would then bring her back the docket.

She usually backed the horse photographed in the *Irish Independent.* On one occasion, she backed a horse called Torch Singer in the November Handicap, a shilling each way, and promised me half the prize money if it won. To our surprise, the horse romped in at 40/1. True to her word, she split her winnings with me – an absolute fortune in those days. Her generosity is something I have never forgotten.

The cottages did not have bathrooms and instead had an outside toilet. As a result, families often took their baths in tin tubs of varying sizes in front of the fireplace. On one occasion, there was great attention drawn to our other two celebrities, sisters who lived on the street: they were Theatre Royal dancers, Royalettes. The story went that one of them had been taking her bath in front of the fireplace when she looked up to see the curtains pulled back and the face of a man peeping in at her. This was an easy thing to do: all that was required to see right into the dining room was to stand on the window ledge and pull back the curtains. All hell broke loose; a vigilante group was set up to patrol the street at night to catch the peeping Tom. We children were only vaguely aware of all these happenings, but we did hear that somebody was caught. We never find out who he was, or what happened to him.

Two Protestant families lived in our area, the Gambles and the Evans. I was very friendly with both of them, particularly the Gambles. I played table tennis in the Gambles' house. When we'd finished playing, we always got a glass of milk and the most beautiful home-made cake. These families always appeared to me to be different from the rest of us. I didn't know why but, looking back on it, they seem to me to have been more Christian and understanding than us Catholics. I travelled with the families to the Boys' Brigade on a Saturday and to their various activities. It was unfortunate that, at this time, we were being taught in school that all Protestants were doomed to go to hell and could never get to heaven!

Every Sunday morning, the Garda recruits who were stationed in the depot just inside the gates of the Phoenix Park marched to Aughrim Street Church to attend ten o'clock Mass. The whole centre part of the church was given over to the recruits, who would march in full uniform, including white gloves, led by the Garda Band. After Mass, they would line up on the roadway outside the church and would drill and exercise there before marching back behind the band to the park, followed by every kid in the neighbourhood, including me. When the Garda training facility was transferred to Templemore, all this free entertainment disappeared, and Sousa's marches no longer featured in our lives.

During the summer months, as we got older, we would all head out at 6 AM on what we called the Strawberry Bus to Lamb's Fruit Farm in Malahide to pick strawberries. We earned five or six shillings for the day's work. In addition to the few bob we earned, we were allowed to eat our fill of strawberries. This seemed at the time to be a stupid decision by the employer, but by the time ten o'clock in the morning came we had eaten enough and were on the verge of getting sick. Often, we returned home in the evening unable to stand up straight, having been bent over all day long – something that prepared me for work at the Brewery.

There were allotments – called plots – at the top of Ross

Street, on the land where O'Devany Gardens now stand. This was a large area where individuals rented allotments and grew their own vegetables, lettuce and potatoes, which they then sold on Saturday to the occupants of the neighbouring houses. The two cottages at the top of Ross Street automatically qualified for a plot, as the plots were attached to the side entrance of their houses.

Looking back on those days, I realise that, although I was never hungry, food was an issue in my young life. I have a clear memory of my father arriving home from Guinness for breakfast at nine in the morning, after starting work at 5 AM. I can still remember how good the fried egg and rasher he shared with us tasted. I suppose the fact that we grew up during the war years and suffered rationing made us conscious of food and how scarce it was at the time.

The radio played a major part in our lives. A gang of us listened every Saturday morning to the omnibus edition of *Dick Barton, Special Agent,* featuring Snowy and Jock. We regularly sat in silence in somebody's small hallway listening to the radio, which was turned up and blaring away in the dining room. On one winter night, when my parents were out, my sister Kalleen and I were listening to *Paul Temple,* a detective story on the radio. On the show, he entered a bedroom and opened a wardrobe, which creaked dramatically. Suddenly, there was a terrible thud and a body fell out. Terrified, my sister Kalleen and I shot out of the house. We were still standing outside in the road when my parents returned. We refused to go back into the house until they had examined it in detail to make sure there was nobody inside. It all seemed so real to us, such was the power of radio – and a fertile imagination!

The sponsored programmes on the radio also influenced our lives greatly and affected our mood on the day, depending on the programmes that were featured during our lunch hour from school. We had *Imco* on Friday, *Prescotts* on Thursday, *Hospital Requests* on Wednesday, *Donnelly Sausages* on another day, and the terrible *Walton's* programme on Saturday. All of the programmes played some pop music, but *Walton's* was all Irish music, and we weren't very patriotic when it came to music! Of course, Sunday night was brilliant because we listened, through the crackle and interference, to Radio Luxembourg's Top Twenty.

In between all these we had Frankie Byrne on *The Jacobs Programme* dealing with everyone's problems. Her catchphrase was: 'These problems may not be yours today, but they may be some day.' As we went into our late teens, we all listened attentively to this programme, particularly to the romantic problems, in the hope that some day we might have that kind of excitement in our lives!

We also spent a lot of time reading and swapping comics: the *Dandy, Beano, Hotspur, Wizard, Eagle* and, of course, the *Champion.* These comics featured characters such as Wilson the runner, who trained up the mountains for the Olympics and then came down to run in his bare feet and win the gold medal. Rockfist Rogan and Danny of the Dazzlers, featured in the *Champion,* were other heroes of ours. Danny of the Dazzlers could take free-kicks which looked to be going wide but would hit the corner flag and then bounce into the top of the net, leaving the goalkeeper wrong-footed. Imagine what he would be worth today in the Premiership!

My first school, which I started at the age of four, was Stanhope Street Convent. In our area, some lads were sent to Stanhope Street, and others went to St Gabriel's. I don't know why, but there seemed to be a perception that children from the more genteel families went to Stanhope Street Convent and the harder nuts went to St Gabriel's.

In Stanhope Street, my life was dominated by Sister Stanislaus, who wore blue glasses and was extremely kind. She devoted a lot of time to the children in the school, taking a personal interest in her pupils. On the other hand, Sister Brigid, the head nun, was a hard woman and likely to dish out punishment. One of her favourite punishments was to send young boys of four or five up to the girls' school to sit in the middle of fifty or sixty girls as a punishment. Needless to say, on such occasions the victim would be roaring crying. Strange how things change: in later years, boys would have seen this not as a punishment but as a treat!

In my first year at school, I was taught by a Miss Lowry, whom I blame for destroying any potential artistic talent in me. When I was four years old, she was teaching the class to cut out the shape of a gansey (sweater) from a newspaper, and I failed miserably to complete the task. She decided to keep those of us who were unable to cut the gansey out of the newspaper hard at it as the clock approached three o'clock. Needless to say, the tears were flowing at this stage, but they were flowing, unfortunately, onto the newspaper, which was becoming more smudged and soggy as each minute passed, thus making it impossible for me to cut anything of any substance or shape out of it. Eventually, Miss Lowry dismissed us with a wave of her hand as being useless. The four of us shot out the door and into the playground with the tears pouring down our faces, feeling like complete failures! To this day, I am unable to produce anything creative, whether it be drawing, painting or anything else. Perhaps conveniently, I blame Miss Lowry.

In May, in Stanhope Street, processions took place around the school grounds and school grotto. The boys who were altar boys were expected to wear their soutanes, and the girls who had made their Holy Communion wore their dresses.

We made our First Holy Communion in the little church in Stanhope Street Convent, a beautiful place of tranquillity. We had earlier been through several trial runs of our First Confession, with Sister Stanislaus acting the priest in the confessional. We all had to produce sins for the trial run. I think most of us arrived with the same batch: 'I stole sugar', 'I was rude to my parents', 'I told lies' – the standard stuff for First Confession.

In Church Street, I joined Brother Joachim, who was constantly on the lookout for altar boys to serve Mass for the Capuchins. He taught Latin for Mass by gently tapping the thin rope around his waist on our heads while reciting *'Ad Deum qui laetificat iuventutem meam.'*

One of the great perks of serving was the ringing of the bell for Benediction. We were so small that we had to be lifted up to the rope. We then hung on for dear life, going up and down on the rope. The priest celebrating Benediction usually had goodies in the pocket of his habit for us after the ceremony. Much to my mother's delight, I served my first Mass on her birthday, Halloween, 31 October.

Living around Oxmantown Road, we were extremely lucky to have one of the greatest amenities in the country right on our doorstep: the Phoenix Park, the largest enclosed park in Europe. As we got older, most of our time – when we weren't playing on the road – was spent there, either in the flower gardens or play-ing football beside the cricket pitches along the main road of the park, using our coats as goalposts.

On one of our many family walks in the park, my father pointed out to me the plaque on the main road that marked the spot where the British Chief Secretary for Ireland, Frederick Cavendish, and the Undersecretary, Thomas Burke, had been murdered. My father told us the story of the subsequent betray-al, by a man called Carey, of the people who had perpetrated the murder, and the fact that Carey had been followed to South Africa, where he was shot on the ship a day before reaching Cape Town. This, my father explained to me, was where the term 'being a carey', meaning 'to betray your friends', came from.

As kids, we would all attend the regular band sessions which were held in the bandstand in the hollow in front of the Zoo during the summer. We spent one fascinating summer harassing an American religious group that brought sick people up on to the stage and prayed over them, and then claimed that they had performed miracle cures. To us nine- and ten-year-olds, intent on mischief on the top of the hill, none of the cures seemed impressive enough to convince us that they were for real, so we gave vent to our feelings before being chased away.

During the bright nights of the summer, we all congregated beside the Civil Service Cricket Ground to play football. Night after night, we played as if we were in Wembley Stadium, and then ran home, with sweat pouring off our foreheads, to be back by the appointed time of nine o'clock. Failure to arrive home on time meant being grounded for a week.

Another area of the Phoenix Park where we spent a lot of time was the Fifteen Acres, where all the playing pitches and dressing rooms were located. All the young schoolboy teams played in the Fifteen Acres. I still have very formal letters signed by Mr Jim Tunney, Secretary of Munster Victoria, telling me that I had been honoured by selection at under-twelve level and to report to pitch No. 26 in the Fifteen Acres the following Saturday.

The Polo Grounds, and the introduction of polo, was a late addition to our lives. We never really got to grips with it or became part of the scene, however. It appeared to be only for posh people, and we stayed away. I'm sure the polo people were relieved! Possibly because we had to pay to go in, the Zoo also didn't feature greatly in our lives either: I can't remember being there many times as a child.

Every afternoon during the summer, young children and their mothers adjourned to the upper level of the flower gardens in the park. The children played hide-and-seek and Cowboys-and-Indians in and out of the bushes, pretending that the upturned metal chairs stuck together were railway carriages on a journey through the Wild West. Our mothers sat knitting and talking as we had our picnics of milk and bread on the grass. We would all stay there until dark, when we trundled home tired but happy.

When one thinks of the current fears in relation to the safety of children, it is strange to look back on that time, when we, as very small children, could wander in and out of bushes and woods, with absolutely no concerns at all. In fact, when my youngest sister, Mary, was born, after a gap of eleven years, my mother, blazing a trail for equality and in order to emphasise that men should have the same responsibilities as women, insisted that I regularly wheel her to the park in her pram. As a young boy of twelve, the thought of bringing a pram to the park did not fill me with joy. Despite the fact that most of my pals tagged along, we were embarrassed going along the North Circular Road wheeling the pram. Once we got inside the park gates, we dumped the pram, complete with baby, in the bushes and went off to play football for an hour or two, collecting the pram on the way back. My mind boggles when I think of what could have happened, or the consequences for me if anything had happened to her during this time.

It certainly was a period of great innocence. Life appeared to be very calm and pleasant, with very little stress, for us kids, even though our parents were probably struggling to keep us all afloat. During and after the war things were very difficult, with rationing, and a scarcity of many essentials. I did not see a banana until I was about twelve years of age. My father cut turf on the Dublin Mountains during the war to keep us warm in the winter. The main road of the Phoenix Park was piled high on each side with turf, put aside by the government for an emergency.

Another feature of the war years was the 'glimmer man'. He was a Gas Company official who went around on a yellow bike checking that no one was using their gas cooker outside the allotted hours. He would come into any house and check to see if it had been used by putting his hand on the gas ring to see if it was warm. Any use of gas outside the specified time period resulted in the gas to the offending household being cut off. Although the use of electricity ended the days of the glimmer men, they are remembered in the name of The Glimmer Man pub in Stonybatter.

Money was tight in our house. My father was paid every Thursday, so by the time Monday came around, my mother was usually struggling. We would be reduced to mince on Tuesday or a rabbit on Wednesday, and the quality of the lunches would diminish as the week went on.

My father worked hard during these years, often from six in the morning until one o'clock the next morning. He usually came home for breakfast and sometimes for lunch, but my recollection was of him either going to or coming from work. He didn't have a lot of time with us during the working week. Every summer, though, we would take half a house in Bray, County Wicklow, and have time together as a family.

Bray at this time, before the era of cheap Continental package holidays, was a huge tourist attraction, especially with the Scots, who came in their thousands. There was entertainment along the seafront, including a variety show and a talent contest. Deckchairs were laid out for the audience in front of the stage at a penny a show. It was usually packed inside the railings in the chairs, even though the show could be seen for free if you stood outside. Paying to see the show had an air of snobbery about it. One year, Elsie Toner, one of the girls staying in our rented holiday house in Bray, went on to win the talent competition, singing 'The Miller's Daughter'. I think she won a shilling or half a crown. We all adjourned to Mezza's ice-cream parlour, where she offered her winnings to the owner, saying we would all keep eating ice cream until the money ran out. It was one of the most delightful days of my life as a child. Years later, when we worked together in Guinness, I often reminded Elsie of the night we spent in the ice-cream parlour.

In addition to the family holiday in Bray, I often went to stay with my grandmother and Auntie Cathy when they had their holidays in Bray. On those occasions we would stay in the amusement arcade until one o'clock in the morning, while my grandmother, seated in the same seat every night, played 'pongo' (now known as bingo). Despite the fact that we were all up so late, the three of us would still be walking on the beach at six o'clock the following morning.

Another place we liked to go to was Roscrea Monastery in Tipperary. My father had forged the initial link with Mount St Joseph's, Roscrea, through Guinness contacts, as had many other Guinness people. These links were based on the fact that one or two of the monks had friends and relations in Guinness. I suspect that Roscrea was also used by some people with a drink problem to dry out. Guinness certainly had its own problems in this regard. On weekend retreats in Rathfarnham Castle, the Guinness contingent would have their cases searched to ensure they had no 'largers' – free bottles of Guinness – stashed away.

We initially went to Roscrea on day trips once or twice a year. It was a magical place for us kids as we grew up. The monastery also had a special significance for my parents: the monks had given them a meal there on their wedding day – after their wedding breakfast at the Dolphin Hotel in Dublin!

We would head down in a car hired for the day, with Fred and Mai Carroll, friends of my father and mother. We always went there in the winter, because it was cheaper to hire a car at that time of year. Many of the cars my father hired were falling apart. On one occasion, the window was missing on one side, and another time the doors were held closed by being tied together with pieces of twine.

My father was usually at his wits' end trying to hire a car to take us on these excursions. Sometimes, the car was hired from a colleague in the Brewery: it probably cost him a small fortune in those days. We would wait at home on the morning of the trip, having been unable to sleep all night, in great anticipation of the arrival of the car to take us to the country. Occasionally, my father would run into difficulties, time would drag on, and gloom would set in, with the possibility that the car might not arrive. There was nearly always a hiccup before we left, but eventually the problems were sorted out and off we headed to Roscrea. We had many a treacherous journey on icy roads in the depth of winter.

In addition to the winter visit, we began to go to Roscrea in the summer, sometimes staying for a week. Women were not allowed to stay inside the walls of the monastery; accommodation for them was provided in a house a hundred yards outside the gates.

Life was very strict for the monks, who lived under a vow of silence and were allowed to go home only every seven years. They set out walking to work on the farm at five o'clock in the morning and returned at dusk. It was a fabulous sight to see all the monks – and there were a lot of them in those days – coming down the road, carrying their pitchforks on their shoulders and with their hoods up over their heads.

The monks had a model farm on the monastery land, where I spent a lot of my childhood days working and helping to bring in the hay on the bogies. (Bogies were flat wooden horse-drawn drays. The bogie was lowered down to ground level, a rope was put around the hay stack, and a ratchet was used to pull the stack onto the platform – similar to a car-recovery operation.) I was allowed do this because of my father's close friendship with Brother Finbarr, after whom I was named. Brother Finbarr had access to the orchard, adjoining the monastery, which was surrounded by huge walls and was something of a secret garden. He brought me in through the large wooden gate using his big key and filled the pockets in his robe with apples and pears, which he later gave to Kalleen and me.

In those days, Mount St Joseph's Church was divided, with the front part of the church being used by the monks to celebrate Mass and to chant, while the back part was used by the public. The inner area, their living quarters, was not open to the public, but males were allowed to enter on occasions. No female was allowed inside the barrier – with the exception, according to my father, of the first lady of the land, the President's wife. The idea of a woman president was never even considered in our conversations.

Lunch and dinner for guests were served in a large room to the right, as you entered the main hall. There was a long table where everyone sat. As they dined, they listened to a priest, who sat to the side of the table and read extracts from the Bible. My recollection is of large bowls of really floury potatoes, and the silence of the diners. Out through the window of the dining room, the river at the back of the monastery could be seen meandering its way for miles through the fields. The tranquillity and beauty of the monastery was magical.

I suppose we loved Roscrea because it got us out of the city and gave us an idea of what it was like to live the country life and to experience the open spaces and peace of the abbey. My parents never lost their love for Roscrea, and in their latter years we often took them down for a day visit when they relived their memories, sitting on the seat facing the monastery with their backs to the orchard. It is strange that, over the years, we have taken so many photographs of our family on the same seat. You can see the ageing of my parents from their youth, through parenthood, and on into old age, all through photos taken in that spot.

In the summer of 1953, my father hired a caravan for our holidays. It was a terrible brown colour and looked like a horsebox. It was great for us kids to be sleeping and eating in this moving house. We were so thrilled that we persuaded my parents to stop on the Curragh for lunch as we travelled to our destination of Rapla, County Tipperary. After lunch, we washed up and set the table for our next stop! Needless to say, when we opened the door of the caravan later, everything was smashed to pieces. It was on this trip that we became friendly with the Gaynors, later of Tipperary hurling fame – a friendship that has continued over the years.

Because we lived in Cowtown and my grandparents lived just across the river in Thirlestane Terrace, off Thomas Street, we would cross the Liffey to visit my granny three or four days a week, and always on Sunday morning. During the war, an air-raid shelter stood outside her house. It was a big cement monster with two entrances, and the inside was dirty and completely dark. It was a place we avoided.

On our journey to my granny's, we always tried to cross the Liffey when a Guinness barge was going up or down. We would immediately look to see if it was Uncle Eddie, Gay Byrne's father, who was a skipper on the barge. If it was his barge, then when the funnel went down to pass under the bridge, he would smother us all in smoke – much to our delight. Eddie was one of the nicest people I met as a child. I still remember with great affection him looking after us in his house on the South Circular

Road. He always made time for the children whenever we visited.

On winter afternoons after trundling over the Liffey from school to my granny's, she would sit in her big armchair singing songs, including 'Three Blind Mice', in the light of the fire as the darkness closed in. On most Saturdays, I was there for lunch, which was usually rabbit stew, thickened slightly with flour. Alec, my mother's brother, and Teddy Balfe, the husband of my mother's sister, Dorrie, called in at lunchtime, as it was a half-day in the Brewery. While it was never clear why, things seemed to be different on Saturday lunchtimes: my grandmother and my Aunt Cathy would fuss around the men as if they were royalty. Even I was aware that they were different, but I didn't know why. Years later, I wondered if it was because they were on the 'Staff' in the Brewery: status levels extended even into Guinness families.

My grandmother and Gay Byrne's mother were sisters, and my grandfather and Gay's father were brothers: two brothers married to two sisters. One of the traditions that my grandfather and Gay's father had was that they both prepared lunch in their respective households on Sundays. I remember calling to Aunt Annie's and seeing Uncle Eddie cutting and cleaning the cabbage, and it was the same in my grandmother's every Sunday. All this despite the fact that both men worked extremely long hours all week, in jobs that were quite physically demanding. Nevertheless, when it came to the weekend, my grandmother just sat in her big chair and reigned like a queen.

My grandfather drove a horse named Roy as a drayman for Guinness. He graduated from horses and carts to motorised lorries. I remember the shock when I heard that my grandfather had broken his arm when the lorry 'kicked him'! It happened when he was using the cranking handle to start the motor.

My grandfather was known as 'Win the War', which I presume stemmed from the fact that he went to fight in the First World War, along with his six brothers. Remarkably, they all returned, although I believe a couple of them subsequently suffered from the after-effects of gas. Unfortunately, my education in the Christian Brothers gave me a very negative outlook on anyone who had anything to do with serving the Empire, and I spent a lot of my time criticising my grandfather for having fought in the war. Indeed, I remember as a child on many a Sunday evening playing cards in my grandmother's, giving him cheek and getting away with it. The women of the house, my aunt and my grandmother, would stick up for me, when in fact I probably deserved a clip on the ear. When my grandfather collapsed and died in 1962, in his pocket was an envelope with £4 and a note saying it was for a wedding present for me.

Christmastime in my grandmother's was brilliant, apart from the fact that my posh cousins the Byrnes, who attended Belvedere College, appeared every Christmas Day. They wore smart blazers and were greeted like long-lost relations – much to the disgust of my sisters and me. This annoyed us greatly: we were there three or four times a week, and yet when they arrived everything seemed to stop for them. We disliked them intensely on these occasions, although in the years that followed, Desmond, Donal and I worked closely together in the Brewery.

There was a constant smell of baking in my grandmother's, particularly at Christmas, when she baked several puddings and Christmas cakes. Everybody seemed to get a cake or a pudding. Her whole dining room would be littered with them, placed all around on beautifully decorated tables. For weeks before, the house would be full of steam as the puddings, in calico bought in Frawley's, boiled away.

As children, we hated having to pack our toys in the afternoon of Christmas day and walk across the Liffey to my grandmother's, returning at one or two in the morning in the freezing cold. Every year, my parents would defend this decision by saying that this might be the last year my grandparents would be there, and that we should make the effort. Year after year, we trudged across, believing that this could be the last. To us, Christmas night was an adult night in my grandmother's, and children were in the way.

The area from Christ Church to James's Street was a mixture

of poverty and traces of affluence. The affluence centred mainly around families who had someone working in Guinness or Jacob's. At the other end of the spectrum, many children around the area went barefoot. The class difference even spread into the church: in John's Lane Church, people sitting in the centre of the church were expected to put sixpence in the plate going in, whereas those in the side pews were expected to put in only a penny.

A key person in my life was my Auntie Cathy, with whom I had a very special relationship. Though I say so myself, Auntie Cathy adored me! I benefited from this adoration for sixty-three years of my life, until she died in March 2002. In fact, within two weeks of her death I was seriously ill in hospital myself. My wife Anne thought that Auntie Cathy was sending for me, as she couldn't bear to be without me and have someone else sharing me!

Cathy herself had been very ill as a child and often repeated the fact that the doctors advised her parents not to bother too much about her education, as she wouldn't live long! When she died, she was only two months short of her ninetieth birthday. Cathy had remained single all her life: she used to recount how she first went out with my father, Jack, before he married my mother, and also with another brother-in-law, Teddy, before he married her sister, Dorothy. Cathy was devoted to the care of her parents – my grandparents – Richard and Kathleen Byrne, who lived in Thirlestane Terrace, just beside the Brewery.

Cathy worked in the Irish Sweepstakes – as many of the ladies of her era, including my mother, did. They were shamefully exploited over the years. When she retired, her pension was the princely sum of £200 – not per week, or even per month, but per *year*. This, while the Sweep made millions for some.

She often told of how she would make it home from Ballsbridge in her lunch hour, taking the tram part of the way and running the rest, to ensure the smooth running of the home. Luckily for me, from the minute I was born she 'adopted' me and looked after me like a second mother. She used to walk me from Thirlestane Terrace to Mount Argus in my pram and lay me on brown paper, so that I wouldn't catch cold, on the grave of Father Charles – now Blessed Charles – to bring me special blessings. She even fell out permanently with one of her friends, who said I looked very small for my age! As I grew older, she brought me to every blessing of the throat on St Blaise's feast day, because I had a dodgy throat, and we walked the Seven Churches every Holy Thursday. She also brought me to walk in all the May processions in Dublin. We went on the mystery train many Sundays and even went regularly to the horse racing in Baldoyle.

It was Cathy who gave me my love of football. She herself was besotted with it. Somebody once told her father that she shouted from the stands like a docker – much to her mother's disgust! She walked me all over the town to the various football grounds – Dalymount, Milltown and Tolka Park – lifting me over the stiles and buying programmes for me. We followed the Transport in one of their Cup exploits all over the country, and she always managed to have two tickets for the front row of the stand for the Cup Finals in Dalymount.

When I was playing myself, she never missed a match. She hurled abuse from the sidelines at anyone who came in to tackle me. She was notorious in Tolka Park: my sisters, Kalleen and Mary, refused to sit with her. After every match, she bought any photo of me that had appeared in the paper from the news-paper's offices.

In later years, when she lived alone, her house was awash with photos of me from birth up through all the stages – much to my embarrassment with my other cousins! When she died, she had hundreds of press cuttings from my various careers, along with another few hundred of her godson, Gay Byrne.

Looking back on it, it was a great comfort to be loved so unconditionally all my life. Although I tried to phone her or call in as often as possible, inevitably I didn't do either as often as I should have. But she never seemed to take offence and would never admit to others in the family that I had any shortcomings!

When the time came to clear her house after her death, it was a sad time indeed: the end of a very happy era. The house had been in our family for sixty-five years. Cathy's neighbours Jean and Michael Whelan, and their family, and Molly and Harry Kielty, made her latter years so much easier, and I am forever grateful to them for that.


The centrepiece of our existence in Cowtown was the Broadway Cinema, known as the Manor, in Stoneybatter. The cinema, at the end of Aughrim Street and Prussia Street, dominated the street, with about forty steps leading up to it. There were cushioned seats at the back and wooden seats, known as the 'woodners', in the front. The 'woodners' cost fourpence a seat. The 'cushioners' were dearer – although, never having paid into them, I don't know what they cost.

Sometimes on a Saturday, big queues would form for the matinée. If you were lucky enough to be at the back when all the 'woodners' were full, you might be allowed into the 'cushioners' for the same price. In many ways, the Manor Cinema was in business terms the Ryanair of its time: their philosophy was 'bums on seats'.

Every Saturday, in addition to the main feature, part of a film was shown, with another part the following week. This was known as a 'follier upper'. The film always finished at a critical stage, leaving us gasping and waiting for the next episode the following week. Of course, everybody returned. The fate of the good guy, 'the Chap', who looked to be in mortal danger, was always the topic of conversation from one Saturday to the next.

How you fared in the Manor on a Saturday, or whether or not you got in, could influence your whole week. Bob, the chief usher, was known by everyone, and he ruled with an iron fist. He regularly walked the queue, and if anybody was caught messing they could be barred for a month. That made you a social outcast: you wouldn't be able to discuss the happenings in the film, and life became pure misery.

The fourpence you needed to get into the Manor was a lot of money at the time. All types of devices were used to obtain this money, including running messages for neighbours or selling jam jars to Dansky, the rag-and-bone man, in Brunswick Street. Dansky collected odds and ends for recycling and would pay one penny for a small jam jar and two for a large one, or a lemonade bottle. He also bought old clothes and paid on the weight of the clothes in the bag. Unfortunately, Dansky became wise to the trick of loading the pockets of the clothes with stones.

On one particular occasion, my grandmother had a clear-out and I brought a heavy bag to Dansky. He was immediately suspicious and emptied the bag on the scales in front of me and my pals. To my horror, out fell my grandmother's corset, complete with huge metal pins. Needless to say, Dansky refused to pay. I couldn't get out of there fast enough.

I became engrossed in football from an early age, probably because, from the time I could walk, my Aunt Cathy brought me to the matches. I was playing for Munster Victoria when I was about ten years of age. We went on an Easter trip to Liverpool. We paid a shilling a week to a fund collected by Mr Jim Tunney, who was the club trainer–organiser–secretary–manager. Many schoolboy teams had outings at Easter, but ours was the envy of others.

One year, we travelled to Goodison Park to see Everton play. On that particular trip, something happened that was to change my life. I was playing inside right at the time, but when we went into the post office to post cards back home, the postmistress got chatting to four of us and decided to guess what positions we played. She commented that I must be the goalkeeper, due to my lanky frame. This set me thinking. It seemed like a good idea, and from the moment I returned to Dublin I was a goalkeeper!

Around this time, two men who were to influence my life greatly, Jimmy Lynch, who worked in Lipton's, and Maurice Fitzsimons, a bus conductor, set up Kirwan Rovers in the area, and I began to play for them. These men were funding the club from their own pockets and, in addition, Jimmy Lynch went so far as to hire a clubroom in the basement of a house in Mountjoy Square. He managed to buy a table-tennis table and created a social club for us, where we met most evenings.

Jimmy Lynch had a major influence on me, especially in terms of setting standards and living life to the best of my ability. He always believed in treating people fairly and he led by example. He ruled our club with firmness and yet we always had tremendous fun and were extremely happy. He taught us how to play table tennis. One year, he, Jimmy Skelly and I won Division 5 of the Dublin and District Table Tennis League and Cup after practising night after night in the basement in Mountjoy Square.

The time given by people like Jimmy Lynch to the development of young people by encouraging and supporting them, and most of all by being available to them, has always been ignored by society. They were very often closer to the young people than their parents when it came to many important aspects of their young lives.

My days of playing table tennis in Mountjoy Square with Jimmy Lynch and football for Kirwan Rovers ended when I signed for Shamrock Rovers minors. Jimmy Lynch continued advising me for many years, though.

My mother and father 'walked out' together from the age of fourteen. My father, Jack Flood, was an altar boy in John's Lane Church, and my mother, Eva Byrne, was in the choir. She always boasted that my father had won her in a fight and in the process had broken one of his fingers. They had very different personalities but were completely devoted to, and dependent on, each other. They came through some very tough times together. In many ways, my father was a difficult man to understand or get close to, but my mother made tremendous allowances for his mood swings. She always balanced them out with what she said were the good things he did, and the good times they had together. She always maintained that he had had little love in his life as a child, his mother having died when he was three years of age.

My father idolised my mother, and in her final years, when she was suffering from Alzheimer's disease and lived in a nursing home in Ratoath, he travelled every day to see her. He would have his lunch and a jar in the pub opposite and then sit with my mother all afternoon, before heading back home to Raheny. The nuns usually gave them tea and biscuits in the visitors' room. The two of them would often fall asleep on the settee with their heads touching.

From what my father told me, their early life together was dominated by walking around Dublin because they had little money. There wasn't a street in Dublin they hadn't walked at some stage.

My mother's family, the Byrnes from Thirlestane Terrace, did not approve of my father and were completely against her marrying him, although my grandmother did in later years say that my mother had 'married a treasure'. My grandmother had aspirations for my mother to marry nothing less than a clerk from the Brewery. My uncle Alec Byrne – my mother's brother – was a clerk on the staff, along with my Uncle Teddy (Balfe), who married my mother's sister, Dorrie. This set the standard.

My mother went ahead regardless; her family did not attend the wedding. I suspect that her sisters were too terrified to go against my grandmother's wishes. The early years of their marriage were a struggle: they had little money and used orange boxes for furniture. My father called to the Dolphin Hotel the day after the wedding to see if there was any refund on drink that had not been consumed at the wedding. Despite this, my mother had elements of snobbery about her that came out over the years, particularly when she was on the telephone. Her voice would change to what we laughingly called her telephone voice.

As a child, my mother spent a lot of time in Rialto, with her Auntie Annie and Uncle Eddie, and she was extremely close to them. In those days, it was not unusual for one child in a big family virtually to live with an aunt and uncle. My mother's aunt and uncle seemed to have taken to my father, who thought the world of them right up to the time they died. He, being a DIY enthusiast, did little jobs for them; I suppose he was trying to repay their kindness.

Uncle Eddie was one of nature's gentlemen, and my sister Kalleen and I loved him dearly. When we visited his house, he made a great fuss of us children, even though the normal practice was to relegate children to the background. He always made us feel special. He was someone who put you instantly at ease, and his smile was infectious.

Aunt Annie and Uncle Eddie were the main supporters of my mother and father when they married, and they did everything to help them with the preparations. In fact, Aunt Annie, probably to defy my grandmother, but also because of her high regard for my father, asked my father to be Gay's godfather.

My parents idolised Aunt Annie and Uncle Eddie and were shattered when Uncle Eddie got cancer and died in 1953. Gay's mother's death on Christmas Eve 1964 was another terrible blow to my parents. They were probably the nearest thing to parents my father had known, as both his parents had died when he was young.

Strangely enough, I know very little about my father's parents, as he never seemed to discuss them with me, although he did talk to Mary, my sister, about them. They had lived in James's Street opposite the fountain, but both died young. He had an unusual view of relations, believing that they were trouble and that you should make your own way in the world. He himself practised this to a fair degree – with a few notable exceptions. His brother Hughie, to whom he was very close, lived in Reading in England. Hughie had come home to take him to England after their father's death, but my father wanted to stay in Dublin. We visited Reading regularly in our teenage years. My father was also very close to his youngest brother Willie, who died very early in life. Willie had left the Augustinian Novitiate in Orlagh and subsequently got married. Willa, his daughter, was like a sister to us.

My father was anti-social and tried to discourage most visitors. When we lived in the cottage in Ross Street, if he thought some of the relations were likely to call, and he didn't want to entertain them, he would put the *Evening Mail* in the letterbox, leaving it sticking out and making it look as if no one was at home to take in the delivery. He would then turn out the lights and we would all sit inside in the glow of the fire, whispering, until the visitors, having knocked on the door and discovered, as they thought, that there was nobody in, moved away. As they disappeared down the street, we would listen to the sound of their footsteps fading in the distance. The lights would then be put back on and we could talk normally again. This worked on many occasions, but some people were more tenacious and came back again later. At that stage, my father would have no option but to open the door and, reluctantly, entertain them.

Despite the fact that my father could be very moody, he could also be quite humorous. He was also considered to be extremely helpful and obliging. When he got a bee in his bonnet, there was no holding him, though. He was a small man but had no fear, and held strong views on what was right and proper. He held the Church in high esteem. He was of the old school and believed that the clergy, being the 'management' of the Lord's company, were above reproach.

The only time I saw a dent in this outlook was when the news broke that Bishop Casey had fathered a son. My wife Anne and I were on holidays in Scotland at the time. When I rang home, my father laughingly apologised to me that he had only been a Brewery man, whereas I could have had a bishop as a father! I knew from the conversation that the whole basis of his belief was under threat, and I felt that his attitude to the church changed over the next few years.

My father was a great walker: for years, he used to walk around the Phoenix Park with us in tow. On one occasion, when I was about eleven or twelve, he and I got the bus to Tallaght, then walked up the Dublin Mountains, over the Feather Beds, through Glencree, and down into Enniskerry, and then got the

41

bus home. It was a hell of a walk. But it instilled in me a tremendous love of the Dublin Mountains which I have to this day. The fact that I live there now is a great source of satisfaction and enjoyment. I can just drive up the hill and over the mountains and bring back the memories of the time I walked over the hills with my father. Unfortunately, many Dubliners never get a chance to see the beauty of the Dublin Mountains.

My mother kept a great sense of humour under cover a lot of the time, but my memories of her in my younger days are of someone who was always good for a laugh. She was in awe of my father and tended to suppress her own personality in deference to him. She was conscious that he could be quite difficult and might not talk for up to a week. The silence drove her mad, but it was only in her latter years that she got the courage to rebel against the silent treatment. Indeed, during her time in Ratoath she often talked of leaving him, but she would then say 'Sure I've nowhere to go, and anyway I love him too much and there would be no one to get his tea.'

Before marrying, my mother, like her sister Cathy, worked in the Irish Sweepstakes. In her school days, she was reputed to have been very clever, winning a number of scholarships. As far as I was concerned, she had the ability to see and know everything. Any time I stepped out of line, even when I was out of her sight, she seemed to know. It is only now that I realise that my guilty face probably gave me away!

My mother led a simple but happy life. She was devoted to my father and to her children. For years, she nurtured the dream that I would become a priest! The arrival of my younger sister, after an eleven-year gap, was a shock to Kalleen and me. My mother nearly died in childbirth, and we were farmed out to my grandmother. I can remember sitting on the top of the stairs in my grandmother's house earwigging to snippets of conversation about how ill my mother was and that she might not live through it. I heard my grandmother querying why my mother was even having a baby at her stage in life. My mother made it through, and my youngest sister, Mary, gave my parents a new lease of life. My father doted on her.

My mother's party piece, which she sang with great feeling, was 'Mate O' Mine'. The words aptly describe their life together and my mother's love for my father:

MATE O' MINE

We set out together, mate o' mine,
When youth was in its prime,
Life – the path that lay before us,
Steep the hill we had to climb.
We neither of us knew the road,
How long the journey, great the load,
Nor I to God, the debt I owe,
For you, mate o' mine.
We set out together, mate o' mine,
We wandered road and hill.
Now it's homeward, through the valley,
We must wander, at God's will.
We neither of us feared the gloom,
Love shall light the path we roam,
Should you be last returning home,
I'll greet you mate o' mine.

For his part, my father left no one in any doubt as to how much he loved her. He was fiercely protective of her, and answering her back or cheeking her brought swift retribution. My father recited 'Dangerous Dan McGrew', written by Robert Service, with great gusto, particularly the part that refers to 'the lady that's known as Lou'.

My mother had a close friend, Mrs Elebert, who lived two doors from us in Ross Street, and they went everywhere together. On Friday nights they headed for the Theatre Royal, where they would spend the time laughing at the comedians and singing along as Tommy Dando and his organ, playing 'Keep Your Sunny Side Up', came out of the orchestra pit to ground level. The words of the songs he played appeared on the screen for all to sing. One night, my mother's ticket was pulled out, for her to take part in the 'Roy Croft Quiz' on stage. She answered the questions and won the prize money, and they both went off on the town to enjoy the winnings. It was rare for my mother to have spare cash like that.

My father's career in the Brewery was very similar to my own. He went in as a messenger and worked in the racking shed and Transport Department before going on to the management staff. He believed that he made a major error when he agreed to go from the shop floor onto the staff: he never really trusted the people in the management that he met, apart from a few for whom he had a great regard.

My father played a key part in the changes that occurred in the company in the fifties and sixties. He was a prime mover in the development of the Guinness distribution system at Kingsbridge. He was seen by most workers as a hard but fair taskmaster. My father and I got on quite well, but I suppose I never realised the worry that I caused my parents as I was growing up. A friend, Mick Cullen, once said to me, as we watched our very young children playing, that kids are a worry for life. He reckoned that children take emotionally and psychologically from their parents all their lives. I recently realised how much my father worried about me when I was watching a videotape that he recorded some years ago, many years after his retirement. In this recording, which was produced by one of the Guinness pensioners, Willie Mullen, who went around interviewing various people who had retired from the Brewery, my father was highly critical of the management people that he had encountered during his days in the Brewery. On the tape, he talks about the difficulty of having me in the Brewery with him and being unable to do anything for me in terms of furthering my career. He said that I was a marked man and that the union would have complained if he had done anything for me. In the interview, he said that one of the reasons he had retired early was to give me a better chance of success in the company.

From the time I went into the Brewery in 1953 as a boy, I was known as Jack Flood's son. Over the years, I went from being content to be known as my father's son to resenting the fact that no one seemed to acknowledge me as an individual in my own right. Anytime I stepped out of line, my father's name would be invoked by somebody. My father was right in his assessment that I was a marked man and would only be given credit for my own achievements after he had left the company. This was why I took such satisfaction from my football career: no one could say that anything I achieved there was because I was Jack Flood's son.

While my mother worried about me too, because she thought the world of me and felt I could do no wrong, she was probably less aware of the trials and tribulations I had over the years. My father was much more aware of the pressures in business than my mother was: my mother, being biased, thought that everything I got I was entitled to by right.

My father constantly advised me to keep my thoughts to myself at work, to keep my mouth shut, never to let 'the rest of them' know what I was thinking, and never, ever to 'let the buggers use you'. This advice was constantly relayed to me until the day he passed away. Unfortunately – or fortunately – I didn't listen to him! On Saturdays in later years, we would meet and go to the Dollymount Inn for lunch and a spin in the car afterwards, and I would fill him in on what was going on in my life. He especially loved hearing the news from the Brewery. He still gave me the same advice: keep your thoughts to yourself. Ironically, my father, while he might have kept his thoughts to himself, was always in the thick of things, fighting his corner.

Despite my father's moodiness, he was extremely popular in the brewery. A bit like myself, though, he was more popular at shop-floor level than at top-management level. He had numerous rows and disagreements with senior management, even as a manager himself. As a result, he eventually sought early retirement. It was clear that he didn't see eye to eye with senior management's plans at the time.

Over the years, many of his colleagues have told me what a great man he was and how he helped them through many difficult situations. I think that, in many ways, my father's tolerance and sense of humour were displayed to a greater extent outside the house than in it. We got along very well, and he helped me through many difficult situations. He could be a hard man if his advice was ignored: he would quickly abandon anyone who decided to do the opposite of what he had told them. I inherited many of his traits – some of them good, and many not so good.

My father probably showed the kindest side of himself during the time that my mother had Alzheimer's. For many months, he had been aware of what was happening, before Kalleen, Mary and I really became conscious of it. Life must have been very difficult for him.

When my mother started to show signs of Alzheimer's, my sister Mary persuaded my father to move to Raheny to be near her, so that she could look after them. In the years that followed, until they died, Mary, her husband Bernie, and their children, Eimear, Brian, Colm and John, showed my parents great love and kindness. In a beautiful gesture of remembrance, in July 2005 Eimear married her husband, Brendan, in Kilmacanogue Church, beside where my parents – her grandparents – are buried.

My mother had a number of minor strokes and ended up one Christmas in Beaumont Hospital. She was not expected to last the festive season, and because it was Christmas we had made contact with the undertaker. I sat beside her bed overnight on Christmas Eve and on Christmas Day. On Stephen's morning, she suddenly sat up, looking for her breakfast. When I explained to her where she was and that it was Christmas, she informed me that this was a second Christmas in hospital for her. She had been in hospital having me in 1938!

My mother always wanted to be buried in Kilmacanogue in Wicklow, as her grandparents were buried there. She told us that her grandmother, whom she seemed to be very close to, loved brown sugar and got married very young so that she could have a supply of brown sugar!

Coincidentally, after driving over the Dublin Mountains on

the night of my first date with Ann, my first wife, I called into the parish priest in Kilmacanogue to get his agreement that my mother could buy a grave there. My mother was over the moon and bought a double grave. She travelled out regularly to see her 'property'. She had no fear of dying once she knew she was going to be buried there: she had a great affinity with the place, as her grandparents had lived over the hill opposite. Unfortunately, the first person into the grave was our first child, who was stillborn in February 1964.

When my mother died, my father lost the will to live. In a short period, he seemed to turn his back on the world and decide to die. I never understood how he went from being mildly ill to having to be hospitalised and then dying, all within a few months. There didn't seem to be a logical reason for it; I still feel that I let him down in some way. A colleague of mine, Padraigín Ní Murchú, wrote this poem on his death, and it reflects my feelings:

DEATH AT YEAR'S END

The man who died was old and weak in bed.

That was my Father now.

But the man I miss and yearn for is the strong wilful man who loved life, work, his children, his wife.

The man who gave me life, education, guidance, sometimes orders, but especially the man who gave me the courage and freedom to plough my own furrow.

But that spirit and energy has moved on in the universe, his job completed here.

Unbidden, the sense of loss will come like waves from the sea.

I am grateful for his good life and in time I can be grateful for his good death, recognising the gifts of courage and freedom he left behind for his children and his children's children.

Over the years, during my football and business careers, I never really knew what my parents were thinking. I never knew how interested they were in my life or how worried they were when things went badly for me. I was never aware of them attending my matches, or how much they knew about my football career. Although other people often told me how proud they were of me, I can't recall them ever saying this to me themselves. It must have given my father great satisfaction to see his son as managing director of Guinness, although it was just not the done thing to convey these feelings to your children. Indeed, when I became personnel director, one of my first tasks was to host the Guinness pensioners' Christmas dinner. Thinking my father would be pleased to be there, I rang him to make sure he would come. He informed me that he was too busy painting the house! I suppose, thinking about it now, it worked both ways: children seldom conveyed to their parents how much they were loved and appreciated. My mother's favourite poem probably speaks for itself:

### I Cannot Read My Tombstone When I'm Dead

More than fame and more than money
Is the comment, warm and sunny –
It's the hearty, warm approval of a friend,
For it gives to life a flavour
And it makes me stronger, braver –
It gives me spirit to the end.
If I earn your praise, bestow it!
If you like me, let me know it!
Let the words of true encouragement be said:
Do not wait till life is over
And I'm underneath the clover,
For I cannot read my tombstone when I'm dead.
If with pleasure you are viewing
Any work that I am doing,
If you like me or you love me, tell me now:
Don't withhold your approbation
Till the Father makes oration
And I lie with snowy lilies on my brow;

For no matter how you shout it
I won't see how many teardrops you have shed.
If you think some praise is due me,
Now's the time to slip it to me,
For I cannot read my tombstone when I'm dead.

*

On leaving Stanhope Street, I went to Brunswick Street CBS. Life there was fairly tough. The Christian Brothers operated a tough regime, and physical punishment was the order of the day. They had a leather strap used for beating on the hand. More often than not, though, the very same strap would be used for hitting on the head, legs, arms, or anywhere else they saw fit. Not all the Brothers indulged in this, but it was an accepted part of being in school.

It was probably viewed by many parents as a positive thing that young, unruly boys could be controlled and disciplined. The fact that many of them were getting the hell beaten out of them was irrelevant. If they went home and told their parents, all they got for their troubles was a second helping of the same, for complaining and 'telling tales out of school'.

During my time in 'Brunner', as it was known, I had four years of Paddy Crosbie, later of RTÉ fame, teaching me. He was a unique man in many ways. He was an excellent teacher, and well ahead of his time. He went on to become a radio and television personality, with his own programme, *School Around the Corner*. While he was all this and more, he could also be extremely cynical.

When I was twelve years of age, I went on a scholarship to the Gaeltacht, in Spiddal, County Galway. I got a scholarship there from the Workers' Union of Ireland, my father being a member of the union. I was to be there for four weeks. I started very badly: within a few days of my arrival, I split my head playing hurling and had to be given stitches. But that was the least of my problems: I hated the place from the moment I arrived. It was my first time away from home on my own, and I suffered from terrible homesickness. I was inconsolable. Every day, I tried to get the organisers of our trip to contact my parents and tell them that I wanted to come home, but my pleas fell on deaf ears. No one was allowed to write home without their letters first going through the organisers, so I had to resign myself to staying put.

One evening, while I was out walking, I met a couple from Dublin driving through Connemara. They stopped me to ask for directions. I hit upon the idea of giving them my parents' address and asking them to pass along the message of how miserable I was and that I wanted to come home. My father appeared the following week and took me home by train.

Unfortunately, this led to a new period of misery in my life in Brunner. From that day on, I was ridiculed by Paddy Crosbie as a sissy and someone who couldn't bear to be parted from his mammy. It was devastating for me: my whole life seemed miserable. Although I had never really liked school, this seemed to be the final straw.

It got to the stage where I dreaded Sunday nights. A cloud would descend on me on Sunday afternoon and I was filled with dread, knowing that Sunday afternoon led to Sunday evening, and on to Monday. The bad feelings on Sunday night remain with me to this day, despite the fact that I have been working for fifty years.

Crosser, as he was known, was a remarkable teacher. One scheme he hit upon was to hand out a ring to about ten boys, out of a class of approximately sixty-four. These chosen boys spoke only Irish all the time at school, including sports and break times. If they were heard speaking English by any of the other boys in the class, these same boys could then report them to Crosser, and they could in turn receive the ring for themselves. The boy caught talking English would lose all privileges associated with the ring.

If you were the wearer of a ring and were due to receive a 'biff' – and there were many of them flying around in those days – the first and second times, you could show the ring and be excused. The third time, you received your punishment, and then the cycle began again: for the next two biffings, you would be excused. Not surprisingly, the rings were sought after. It was one of the contradictions about Crosser that he did many things well but could undo it by some cynical action.

The other innovation was that, once a week, on Friday afternoon, he would take the class on various field trips around the city. In the fifties, this was well in advance of what would now be considered the norm. He took it upon himself to take sixty-four young messers around the city!

We visited the Players Cigarette Factory, the *Independent* newspaper's offices, St Michan's Church, and various other places. I think it was an indication of his ability to put the fear of God into people that he was able to take all of us around the city confidently and keep us under control. I would love to see a teacher today take on the same task.

One of the experiences that I remember vividly is our trip to St Michan's. Our group was too big for all of us to go down together to the crypt to shake hands with the Crusader. We were split into groups, and when one group went into the crypt, the others were left to sit in the church with strict instructions to remain quiet.

When my group's turn with the Crusader had finished, we waited in the church. Thinking that Crosser had gone back down into the crypt, I got into the pulpit and proceeded to give a sermon to my classmates. Of course, they all thought this was hilarious. As I looked down at them, however, I suddenly saw their faces freeze in shock. I couldn't figure why – until I looked around, to see Crosser standing behind me in the pulpit. He hit me such a box on the head that I went head over heels down the steps and ended up looking up at him in the pulpit. He then said to me in Irish that he would see me first thing on Monday morning. He duly did – and dispensed his own brand of punishment.

Another innovation Crosser had was that every week he ran a raffle for a prize of a shilling – out of his own pocket. He would hand out numbered tickets as rewards for work well done,

51

such as a good essay, and then on Friday he would draw the winning ticket from the hat. If you were lucky enough to have your ticket drawn, you would be in the money.

Every day, for half an hour, we took time out to tell a story. We all formed an orderly queue and each took our turn. The only condition, of course, was that the story had to be told in Irish. It was a very good idea and encouraged us to develop our skills in the language. Initially, in our innocence we got up and told stories about things we had done, such as breaking a neighbour's window, or playing knick-knock on the doors in our street. These tales were of course unacceptable to Crosser: he would cynically give the storyteller a bonus ticket for the story and then tell them to line up outside for a biffing because of what they had done!

Crosser reigned with a fair amount of fear. This was probably necessary, given that our class of sixty-four was back to back, in the same room, with another class of sixty boys. Compared to the numbers that teachers of today complain about, you can understand the difficulties he faced in keeping control. Without the threat of physical force or corporal punishment, it probably would have been an impossible task to manage our group.

In one particular year, the teacher who taught the other class in our huge room had just been taken on by the Christian Brothers. He had no control over his class, and the boys would run amok in front of his very eyes. On one particular day, he took his greyhound into the classroom, possibly because he had no other place to leave it during the day. He then proceeded to play the violin, as the greyhound sat on a chair listening attentively. The messers in the class had a field day. When the teacher took his greyhound outside to relieve itself, Crosser would step into the breach and put manners on anyone he had observed being out of line. The new teacher would return to a perfectly behaved classroom thinking he had control of the class, while really it was all Crosser's doing.

The only time I saw Crosser on the back foot was the day when he tried to reprimand a boy called, as far as I remember,

Donaghy. The previous day, as he was walking around the class-room, Crosser saw Donaghy rushing out the school gates; as he went, he brushed against Crosser's car. After lunch, Crosser sent for him. When the poor lad came into the classroom, Crosser proceeded to tear strips off the young fellow for bumping his car. As Crosser grew more and more angry, he began to slap Donaghy about the head. Donaghy's natural instinct was to put his hands up to his head to protect himself and to keep backing away. This infuriated Crosser even more: he warned Donaghy to put his hands down, behind his back. As the guy backed away, he came up against the window ledge, where, probably in despera-tion, he grabbed hold of the pole that was used to open the win-dow. In the blink of an eye, he proceeded to hook the pole onto Crosser's trouser belt loop and somehow managed to hoist Crosser about a foot off the ground. Crosser then fell back down onto the floor on his backside, with a thud.

There were gasps of horror from all of us. We were sure that, after that stunt, Donaghy was probably going to be execut-ed at dawn. In fact, he fled the scene: he ran from the room and out the school gate, and was never seen again – although Crosser sent someone to his class looking for him every day.

Crosser, in his wisdom, decided that our class should learn Irish dancing – something that us sixty-four boys wanted to rebel against but were terrified to oppose. Just before the summer hol-idays, we were all entered into the dancing competitions in the Father Matthew Hall in Church Street. I remember lining up my 'Uimhir a trí' on my chest, not having an idea how to put a foot under me. When the winner was called out, it was 'Uimhir a trí'! Although I thought there must be a mistake, up I went to collect my medal – only to discover that the judge was a neighbour of my granny. I never knew whether the medal was suspect or whether I was a better dancer than I thought!

Another of Crosser's initiatives was for everyone in the class to be a character from Irish history. This meant that each of us knew off by heart the story of a particular person. Back then, this approach was quite novel. When we were asked a question on any of these characters, we would turn immediately to the person in the class who had been assigned that character, and all the details would come back to them. I was Olaf Fodhla, a wise man of ancient Ireland.

Science was also a great attraction – being able to experiment with puffs of smoke and explosions of one sort or another. I'm not sure if the science teacher, 'Jock', was any good, or if he was aware of the possible consequences of some of the experiments we carried out. I always had the feeling that we were entering a danger zone when we entered that classroom. It was certainly exciting: one of us could have become the first Irishman to reach Mars!

During one of his talks in class, Crosser made a prediction that in years to come speeches and conversations by people in history would be able to be recovered out of the air through technology. Although this hasn't literally happened yet, a lot of things that *have* happened, such as the Internet, are along similar lines to Crosser's forecast.

When we did the Primary Certificate, I got two hundred in English, Irish and arithmetic: full marks. Paddy Crosbie subsequently wrote a very nice note to my parents congratulating them and pointing out that this was a unique event and that no one would ever be able to beat my score. (I still believe that my getting full marks was some mistake.) He stressed that he thought that I should stay on at school and further my education up to university level – neither of which I did.

When I played for Morton Football Club, I was walking up Manor Street one day when I met Crosser. He asked me if I was this guy Flood who was playing 'that soccer game'. When I replied that yes, it was me, he demanded to know why I would want to do such a thing. I snapped back quickly: 'Purely for the money.' He was disgusted and just turned and walked away. That was probably the one and only time I got my own back on him.

But there was more to Brunner than the teaching. It was a hurling school, with some Gaelic football. For a good hurler, life at school was made a hell of a lot easier. One particular teacher, Mr Brennan, was a fanatical hurling fan and trained the hurling team. Mr Brennan, 'Buller', seldom punished the hurlers for anything. I loved hurling and got a trial to play with the Dublin Schools team, who at that time were about to play against the Belfast Schools.

At the same time as I was playing hurling, I also played soccer. The GAA ban on foreign games was in force at the time, prohibiting anyone who was playing Gaelic sports from playing soccer. Indeed, soccer was outlawed in our school. As a result, I came under fierce pressure to give up soccer, even being suspended from school at one stage for not making myself available for Gaelic games. If I had been allowed to play both sports, I think I might have moved towards hurling as my first preference. The best thing about hurling is that there is seldom the type of narking and rowing that is seen so often in other sports. Probably because it is such a dangerous game, it is more important to stay in control. It's ironic that one of my recent tasks has been to act as independent chairman in the talks between the Croke Park management and local residents: Crosser would have been proud of me!

My last experience of Brunner was at a dinner which was held for past pupils in the school almost twenty years ago. Having arrived in the school, I was directed to the main room and told my table number. Halfway through the dinner, I complained that it was unfortunate that we hadn't been seated with our original classmates, as this would have made things much more interesting. All the mature faces around me glared at me in horror as it was pointed out that these *were* my classmates. I put my head down, dived into the dessert and kept my mouth firmly closed from then on. Age is a terrible thing!

\*

My teenage years were a mixture of enjoyment and misery: enjoyment on the sporting front and misery on the personal front because of my lack of self-confidence. This lack of confidence probably arose because of a combination of my Catholic upbringing, a Christian Brothers' education and working in Guinness. All these situations created a subservient culture, operating as they did in a most authoritarian manner.

Whatever about the quality of academic education provided by the Brothers, they did not prepare us for the real world. Our Catholic upbringing taught us to know our place: to obey authority and the rules, and not to question things. We seldom took chances or put our heads above the parapet, and the few who did usually ended up in trouble. At that time, very few entrepreneurs came out of working-class areas.

The complete absence at school of any training in social graces or mixing with the opposite sex left boys ill-prepared for the problems of teenage years. Even though I was earning good money in the Brewery and had a job that people seemed to think was a good one, I had no confidence at all when it came to girls. To a large extent, this resulted from the fact that I couldn't dance. Anyone who remembers the fifties and sixties knows that it was a period dominated by the dance halls and the big bands. My inability to dance left me well and truly scuppered.

In fact, the only time I ever attempted to dance was for a slow foxtrot – which I found easier than the others. As a result, I had to wait all night for one to be announced. I then had to ensure that I was strategically placed in front of or behind whoever I intended asking up, before I pounced. Most times, these tactics backfired, particularly if, after the slow foxtrot was announced and yours truly had moved in, the announcer said that it was to be a ladies' choice. This happened to me on the night I met my first wife Ann in 1960. Having asked her up to dance and then finding myself stranded, I was relieved when she said: 'I'll dance with you anyway.'

All of the lads I hung around with were good dancers, and one of them, Kevin Nugent, was a brilliant dancer and would dance all night. But my handicap when it came to dancing turned out to be a nightmare for me. It meant that frequently I would spend the whole night at a dance without dancing. Men were expected to dance a number of times with a woman, to build up a relationship with them; then, if possible, the man would invite her for a coffee in the hall, before trying for a date. Unfortunately, in my case I couldn't wait that long. I had to move at the first opportunity and try for a date on the first dance. On most occasions, I was turned down flat because I was perceived to be too forward. Eventually, I lost heart and gave up trying.

There was one period when I went to half a dozen dances in a row and didn't get up to dance once. When I saw the compère going to the microphone, I always started to walk towards the Gents so that, if a ladies' choice was announced, I could proceed to the toilet. If the announcement wasn't for a ladies' choice, I could change direction and make a decision as to whether I was going to try for a dance or not. This had nothing to do with arrogance, or my not wanting to dance: I was dying to dance but didn't have the ability, or the confidence.

We danced in the Crystal Ballroom on South Anne Street on Saturday nights. The doors opened at 7.30 PM for an 8 PM to midnight dance. We would pay, go in, have a look around, see who was in the hall, and then get a pass out to go to Grafton Street.

Most of us didn't drink at the time – not unusual then, for lads involved in sport – but we still liked going into pubs and having soft drinks. My experience, however, was that the people who were drinking very often had a completely different view of the 'talent' that was at the dance after the few drinks. Having initially felt that the talent was 'brutal', they would be raving about the beautiful women in the hall when we came back in. Being cold sober, of course I could see no difference: it was as though we were at two different dances.

In those days, John Clarke, the only black singer in Dublin, was the attraction in the Crystal. He came on at about 9.30 and sang a medley for around half an hour – which usually included a samba, a tango and all sorts of other things. Because it was a medley, I was again restricted due to my limitations when it came to dancing. Sometimes I took a chance when the floor was crowded and would get up, hoping that I wouldn't be noticed shuffling around. Unfortunately, it usually didn't work out that way, and I'd end up sitting down halfway through the dance.

The other problem I faced when it came to dancing was being so tall – six foot one. I hated having to dance or go out on a date with a small woman because it made me self-conscious about my height. In the Crystal, it was particularly embarrassing, as there were mirrors right around the ballroom from halfway up the walls: when you were dancing with somebody small, you looked as though you were dancing on your own!

My obsession about not being seen with a small woman resulted in one calamitous episode after a dance in the Mansion House. As it came to near the end of the night, I was sitting at the back of the hall. I remember that Mick Delahunty was playing. I got talking to a girl sitting in front of me who seemed very nice and made a date to meet her at the Gas Company in D'Olier Street the following Wednesday.

On the night, as I came thundering around the corner to meet her, to my horror I was upon her before I realised that she was only about five foot three. What I hadn't realised was that, in the Mansion House, she had been sitting on the tipped-up seat with her legs dangling, so I had never really seen how small she was. There was no way I was going to walk up O'Connell Street to the Savoy or the Carlton with her. Thinking quickly, I decided we were going to the Regal, which was down the side passageway, beside the Gas Company. We duly arrived at the Regal – I remember that *South Pacific* was on – and were shown to our seats. This girl was so small that on two occasions the usherette showed someone else into the seat, thinking that the seat beside me was vacant! I had identified that she lived in Ranelagh, and when we came out of the pictures I dropped her straight home and said goodbye. To this day, I still feel ashamed about the way I acted with that girl.

Dance halls were all the rage, with Saturday and Sunday

nights being the most popular. There was a proliferation of dancehalls, including the Crystal, the Olympic, the National, Clery's, the Kingsway, the Metropole and the Four Provinces ('the Four Ps'). We danced mostly in the Crystal, and at the Royella, in the CIÉ club in Marlborough Street, on a Saturday night. The Olympic Ballroom was not acceptable in our house: my mother did not approve of it, or the Four Ps, because of the type of people, she believed, who went there. She did accept that the Olympic was all right for the 'Ags' (agricultural students' dance) on Wednesday night – a dance that usually attracted nurses and Gardaí. It was strange that, even at that stage, in our late teens, our parents had such an influence on us.

The Crystal Ballroom had a very strict entry policy: men had to be wearing a tie, or they would not be allowed in. On one occasion, one of our guys, being smart with the bouncer, asked whether, if he came in naked with just a tie on, he would get in. Of course, this resulted in us all being barred for two weeks.

That time was the height of the dance-band era, with Brendan Bowyer, 'Spit on me' Dickie Rock and many others becoming stars overnight. Different dance halls attracted different bands. The Royal Showband and the Melody Aces played regularly in the Crystal, whereas Mick Delahunty played in the Mansion House. Every summer, the Arcadia in Bray had Victor Sylvester, and sometimes Ivy Benson and Her All Girls' Band from the Isle of Man. While it all sounds good, it was sheer hell for me: nobody knew how miserable I was. On one occasion in the Crystal I was standing against a pole when two girls passed by. One of them commented: 'Look at him, he's been holding up that pole for two hours without budging.' That shattered me for weeks.

If a man was lucky enough to get a date at a dance during the week or on Saturday night, he would be expected to get tickets for the pictures on Sunday night. Although every cinema was usually booked out, this excuse would cut no ice with the date: his rating would drop dramatically if he failed to get tickets. As a result, there was a thriving trade in black-market tickets every Sunday on O'Connell Street.

If you had no date and didn't want to go dancing on Sunday, there was always the Olympia. The Olympia had two films on Sunday in place of its stage show. The screen was very small, however, and they sometimes managed to mix up the reels and run the two films into each other. On one occasion, they were showing a war film. John Wayne was spraying bullets everywhere, when suddenly we were presented with a fellow strangling a woman in an attic. Baffled silence prevailed for a few seconds, before the place erupted into laughter and slagging.

Another problem arose because, when someone on the balcony stood up during the film to go to the toilet, they invariably blocked the screen. Howls of abuse would ensue – to which the offender would respond by projecting two fingers in rude gestures onto the screen.

In addition to the normal dances, there were dress dances during the winter months. Dress dances were something special. The sense of occasion – dressing up like film stars, the beautiful clothes, and all that went with it – was magic. The women in their ballroom dresses were collected by car or taxi by the young men in their dress suits, carrying boxes of chocolates.

The men's dress suits were all hired, usually from the Penguin in Abbey Street. The Penguin, when it first opened, gave an orchid for the young lady with every suit hired. For months, anybody hiring a suit there had an advantage over everybody else because women were very impressed at being given an orchid when their young man arrived to collect them. It was only when they subsequently found out that the orchid went with the suit that the brownie points disappeared.

There was no question of the woman making a contribution or paying anything towards the expenses, apart from getting her dress. The tickets and everything else were paid for by the men. This was long before the days of 'going Dutch' or equality. Men were only too happy to pay for the privilege of taking out a young lady.

Around this time, a debate started in the *Evening Mail*, with letters regularly to the editor from men, and women, complaining about the lack of tall partners in the dance halls. The letters from women bemoaned the fact that it was so difficult to find tall men, and the letters from men complained that they were fed up dancing with small women.

An entrepreneur of the day – I think he was a Garda – saw the opportunity in this and hired a dance hall for what was to become known as 'The Tall Girls' Dance'. Despite the name, this dance was actually for tall men as well as tall women.

Entry to this dance was based on height. On the way into the dance hall, people had to touch their heads on a measuring bar that extended from the door. There was one for men and another one for women. Those who didn't meet the required height were refused entry. Nowadays, this would probably qualify for a charge of discrimination. Nobody complained about it then, however, and the Tall Girls' Dance thrived. Every Sunday night, there were long queues right down the road long before the doors opened. This dance ran for many years; its organiser must have made a fortune.

Dances usually finished around twelve o'clock, except on the odd occasion when they were extended to 1 AM – although this was never on a Saturday night. Everyone adjourned to one of the milk bars on the quays or on Bolton Street, for a pint of milk and a 'Russian' – a cake like marzipan – before heading home to bed. On Saturday and Sunday nights, hundreds of people would converge on O'Connell Street around midnight, but there was seldom any trouble.

One of the milk bars we frequented was the Wagon Wheel in Bolton Street. Opposite this milk bar was a big building, four or five storeys high. There always seemed to be lots of activity there every night, with cars and taxis pulling up in droves. Initially, when we watched it from the milk bar, we assumed it was some kind of drinking place. We subsequently found out that the place, called Dolly Fossett's, was a reputed brothel – although most of us didn't fully understand what a brothel was at the time. My last recollection of Dolly Fossett's was reading on the front page of the *Evening Mail* one evening a big banner headline saying: 'DOLLY FOSSETT'S CONDEMNED AS A DANGEROUS BUILDING'. There was no answer to that one!

The Isle of Man was a great holiday venue for Dublin teenagers in the fifties and sixties. The Villa Marina, with Ivy Benson and her All Girls' Band, the Fair Glen, Onchan Head, Douglas Head, and the steam train were all well known to Dubliners. A balance between males and females never seemed to be reached. One year, when there were plenty of men, the men went back and told their colleagues that there were too many men, and women told their friends the good news that there were plenty of men. Then the next year, the balance went completely the other way. The thing was to be there in the right year!

As a teenager, I think that I started to believe in myself as a person around the time I signed for Shamrock Rovers Minors at the age of eighteen. I felt that playing for Rovers gave me status among my peers: Rovers was the top team in the country, and playing for them, even as a minor, made me something special. In my own area, Cowtown, the fact that I was playing in goal for Shamrock Rovers Minors suddenly changed people's attitude to me – or at least I believed it did. Although my difficulties when it came to dancing continued through these years, football started to give me the confidence I needed to develop as a person.

Looking back on my teenage years, which everybody says are the good years, I have to say they were anything but good for me. I hated them and was glad to see the end of them. I had always felt as though I was on the fringes looking in, at the mercy of the slow foxtrot.


Having suffered from a terrible shyness and insecurity in my dealings with the opposite sex, I met Ann Collins in 1961. We had a fairy-tale engagement in St George's Square in Glasgow on Christmas Eve 1962. The snow was falling, and everything seemed perfect. This was during my footballing years with Greenock Morton. The extra money I earned there allowed me to bring back something from every trip for our new home together. Life seemed good.

We were married in April 1963 in James's Street Church. We lived at first in a flat (as they were then called) on Ballymun Avenue. It was while we were living there that our first child, a daughter, Sandra Ann, was born in February 1964 – sadly a stillbirth. The circumstances were tragic and painful. As was the custom at the time, we never saw our daughter, and we buried her in our plot in Kilmacanogue Graveyard, where my parents are now with her. This was a very traumatic experience for us both, but particularly for Ann, who never got over it.

Our son, Barry, was born in March 1965. When we went to christen him, the priest refused to allow us to call him Barry: he said that there was no such saint. So, rather rapidly, we decided to christen him Finbarr Barry John. To this day, he sometimes uses the name Finbarr, although he is known as Barry.

Barry, having left CBS in Monkstown, went to Trinity College to do science, but his heart lay elsewhere, and he changed to archaeology. He went to Edinburgh University to continue his studies and receive his doctorate. It is very strange seeing reference to Dr Finbarr Flood! Barry has a very interesting life, travelling the world in pursuit of his speciality: Islamic art. He is now an assistant professor in the University of New York. He is a master of surviving on very little and making his way around the world as economically as possible.

Suzie was born in 1967. She has had a varied life, working as a chef, an activist and, more recently, a civil servant. She is very interested in social justice and completed a diploma in Development Studies at Kimmage Manor. Her excellent results there qualified her to do a Masters of Science in agriculture, environment and development at the University of East Anglia. Suzie is passionate about the plight of the disadvantaged; in 1999, she travelled to Iraq on a sanctions-busting trip. She is currently studying for a Masters in international relations at Dublin City University.

Ann and I separated in 1983; sadly, Ann died tragically in an accident in 1985. I married again – another Anne, this time with an 'e' – in 1999. We had been together since 1988, but as she awaited the introduction of divorce into Ireland, we made a life together. The arrival of our first grandson, Josh, changed our lives completely. I can well understand people who say: 'If I had known grandchildren were such fun, I would have had them first!'

To Suzie's great credit, she continued her very intensive year of study for her masters while she was pregnant with Josh. She returned to Dublin for his birth and very shortly afterwards went on to complete her studies in Norwich, with Josh at the crèche every day! Joshua Finbarr is now eight years old and has brought great happiness to myself and Anne.

Although Anne had never wanted children of her own, she has taken to the granny role like a duck to water, and we have had great pleasure in taking Josh to our house almost every weekend since he was born. Alex Christopher was a lovely surprise when he was born in April 2003. The two boys' birthdays are only two days apart, so April will be a party month from now on!

Alex was born with a cleft palate, but unfortunately he also had other complications, which have meant he was in Our Lady's Hospital for Sick Children for seventeen months after he was born. He is a lovely child: since being discharged from hospital, he is on the move all the time. Having the Flood brothers is quite a challenge, but one which Anne and I enjoy!

## 2

# THE BREWERY

## MESSENGER BOY TO MANAGING DIRECTOR

My family was a Guinness family through and through. Both my grandfathers and my father, as well as various uncles and cousins, were employed in Guinnesses. As a result, before I went into the Brewery to work, aged fourteen, I knew a fair bit about what went on inside those imposing walls.

From listening to my father, I knew about the Brewery and spent a lot of time standing looking through the gates at the small trains transferring casks around the yard, the lorries being loaded, and pigeons eating the grain which had fallen out of the silos. I kept pigeons at home and watched with envy all that free feed lying just inside the gates, but out of reach.

All around the area where my granny lived, Thomas Street, the smell of the Brewery was a permanent feature. Just up the road at the canal at Rialto, the barges were loaded with barrels to be taken down the canals for distribution around the country.

Down at the bottom of Steeven's Lane, several horses waited all day to be coupled with Guinness horse and drays for the pull up Steeven's Lane. This incline was felt to be too much for one horse.

There was also the Guinness siding on Victoria Quay, where

small-gauge trains coming out from the Brewery offloaded barrels onto the quayside. The barrels were then loaded by crane onto the barges for transportation to Custom House Quay, before being transferred to the Guinness ships going to England.

I had seen the inside of the Brewery before I started work there: as a small boy, I had gone in at Christmas time with lunch for my father. My father ran the Blue Book, a loan system like the Credit Union. At Christmas, there would be a big divvy paid out and my father would have no time to go home to eat. I would be allowed through the gates by the gate man when one of my father's men collected me and brought me to my father. My father would often put me sitting up on the counter in the Blue Book office. This was a great spot for me: everyone who came to do business would drop me a penny or two, and I would come out with my pockets rattling.

I was always conscious as a child of the smell of hops and beer and the thousands of wooden casks piled twenty high in a large yard, waiting to be loaded. For someone so small, it was a fascinating world; as my father was such a key element in it, I felt I was part of it too.

Every year, the Guinness messenger boys' examination was held. The exam was used to help recruit fifty to seventy messengers and laboratory attendants. On a specific day in January, up to five hundred boys would queue down Watling Street and then be allowed in to the Rupert Guinness Hall to sit the exam there. The Guinness messengers exam generated its own cottage industry. At the time of the exam, grinds were provided all over Dublin, just as there are now grinds for the Leaving Certificate.

Sons of employees (known as 'SOEs') were given priority when it came to sitting the examination; after them, those in the highest-level classes in secondary school were selected. Boys who were successful in the exam were notified in February and were called to start work as vacancies arose throughout the year. Successful boys were seen as having made it for life, although my granny went further, saying: 'A Guinness man meant money,

66

dead or alive.' My mother's enthusiasm when I was successful in the messenger examinations was hard to fathom. Even though I now had a pensionable job, I was fifty years away from collecting my pension!

At the time of the boys exam in 1953, I was mad keen to get into the Brewery. This was not because of any grand illusions I had about the place but because it meant having my own money. It appeared to me that those who worked in the Brewery, even if they were only teenagers, had an air of confidence about them. This may have stemmed from the fact that they always seemed to have more money than older boys. They also seemed to be very successful with the local girls. In comparison to those who were still at school – and who as a result didn't really rate in either the financial or the romantic stakes – they were kings.

After I got full marks in the Primary Cert, just before I sat the 1953 Guinness exam, Paddy Crosbie and the Christian Brothers did all in their power to try to convince me to stay on at school and not to go into the Brewery. I remember clearly my father bringing along two people I respected, Joe Patterson and Sean Cromien, who were much older than me and who had been involved with me in the Legion of Mary, to try to persuade me to stay on at school. They failed: there was no way I was going to be stopped. Many years later, Sean Cromien, who went on to become Secretary of the Department of Finance and who had a distinguished career in the civil service, wrote to congratulate me on my appointment as managing director. He commented that he was unsure whether he could claim the appointment as a success or a failure!

At the time, I assumed the opposition to my joining the Brewery, particularly from the Christian Brothers, was because of an anti-drink stance on their part, but years later I came to understand that this was not the only reason. They feared that the best of the boys being taken from secondary schools would be sacked from the Brewery at eighteen or twenty-one years of age, as the company had that option, or that, if they were lucky enough to be kept in employment, they faced a life of labouring work, with no real prospects.

They were right. A lot of young men were indeed laid off at eighteen and twenty-one years of age. When 'boys' (as they were known), aged between fourteen and eighteen, became 'lads' at eighteen, they were usually transferred to the Number-takers Section, or let go. Then, at twenty-one, when they became 'men', they were transferred into the workforce, to labouring jobs. Most of them had to endure extremely bad working conditions, and long hours with no prospects. As a result, many of these people used their skills to fight the system through the union, or by opposing management in general, in later years.

As well as the written exam to become a messenger, there was a medical exam that, while dealing with the person's physical condition, also took into account their height–weight ratio. A graph indicating the required weight for height decided your fate. This was a major problem for me. I was a long string of misery, and my parents realised that, given my height, I would not reach the weight requirement for entry to the Brewery. I was therefore put on a strict regime of a pint of milk a day for more than a year, to fatten me up before I went for the medical entrance exam. Unfortunately, in subsequent years, when I had a kidney stone, I was told that part of the reason for it was drinking too much milk in my youth!

The day I went for the medical exam, my mother, in an effort to keep my weight as high as possible, would not allow me to go to the toilet. After being examined by the doctor, I was sent into an adjoining room with a medical attendant in a white coat. As luck would have it, this man turned out to be Joe Costello, a friend of my father's and a regular visitor to our house. When he saw my weight registering on the scales and took into account my height, he made a quick mental calculation and realised that I was underweight. I heard him mumble under his breath: 'Oh, Jesus.' He then quickly pressed his foot on the scales, winked at me and called out the 'adjusted' weight in stones and pounds. In one bound, I was free from the horror of school and unleashed on the Brewery community.

In subsequent years, I was to remember that day and think of the breaks that come in life, both good and bad – breaks that can make a significant difference to whether a person succeeds or fails. This was my first slice of good luck – thanks to Joe Costello being in the right place at the right time.

The Brewery I joined in 1953 was class-ridden and autocratic. Non-staff people like me had very few rights. We could not complain about the type of work we were asked to do; if we did, we fell foul of our immediate superiors, the men messengers. Several times, I was fined a shilling for 'looking contemptuously' at my superior. He would report me to the head messenger, and that would be that. I had no chance of defending myself. I have often been asked if being fined upset me: the reality is that I would have been very disappointed if my look of contempt had not been noticed. To me, it was a shilling well spent.

When I joined, the Brewery was laid out over more than sixty acres. Within the walls was a self-contained city, with its own catering, medical and recreation facilities. A small power station on the site produced electricity for the Brewery, and even supplied the ESB at times. The different levels of the Brewery were all connected by narrow-gauge railways, which covered a distance of some eight miles and over which small locomotives conveyed raw materials and other goods to various parts of the site, as required. The ascent from the lower level to the upper level was made by several tunnels constructed under James's Street. There was also a cooperage, where wooden barrels were made and repaired by hand, and a large printing department, where nearly two million labels a day were produced. There was a post office, through which 700,000 letters passed each year; the Medical Department, employing doctors, dentists, physiotherapists, chiropodists and a social worker; and a savings bank, a building society and an assurance society run for the benefit of the employees. Also on site was an ambulance service, a uniformed police department, a sports section and recreational facilities, and of course our own fire brigade.

The company had a number of societies to help employees,

including a building society, a mutual-benefit society and a 'bury yourself' assurance society. The Guinness building society gave loans for house purchase at rates less than the going rate outside the company. The mutual-benefit society, known as the Blue Book, was a loan society run on similar lines as the credit unions. It made big payments at Christmas. Everyone who joined the Brewery was encouraged to join the 'Bury yourself for half a crown a week' scheme. The idea behind the scheme was to save enough for a decent suit to be buried in. When you had deposited a certain amount, the deductions ceased and you could relax in the knowledge that you were well prepared for your day out!

Within the organisation, there were clear distinctions between the monthly paid 'staff' and the weekly paid 'workers'. Within the staff, further segregation existed, with No. 1 Staff, No. 2 Staff, Gate Staff, Unclassified Staff and Laboratory Staff, each of which had its own status symbols and snobbery. Over the years, we heard stories of people who were promoted from one group to another being ostracised because the group to which they were promoted did not consider them suitable for inclusion. Most of these groups had their own separate dining rooms, as had the weekly paid workers.

Tradesmen and general workers dined in Belview at the back of the Brewery, in a building known as the Workmen's Rooms. Attached to the Workmen's Rooms was a snooker room and recreation and library facilities. A separate dining room was provided in the building for supervisors and foremen. The messengers dined in a room in the basement under James's Street.

Additional separate dining rooms were provided for the No. 1 Staff, No. 2 Staff, Brewers and Directors. The doctors dined alone in the Medical Department in order, as they put it, 'to consult on key medical issues of the day'.

While there was division and segregation within the management ranks, there were also divisions within the weekly paid workers. The workers tended to divide into three categories: the ex-boys, who had mostly come in through the exam at fourteen and who were mainly Dubs; those who had served in the British army; and the culchies, who had come up from the country with a letter from a priest or bank manager and were taken on by the Brewery.

The tensions between these three groups often came to the surface, especially when, at the age of twenty-one, ex-boys were sent out to work in groups that included both ex-service people and culchies.

The ex-servicemen who worked in the Brewery included people who had been promised jobs if they volunteered to fight for the Empire. Over the years, in homes around the Thomas Street area, I have seen many photographs of young men in uniform who, I was told, were brothers of the elderly residents. They had gone to the First World War on a promise of a job in Guinness upon their return. Sadly, many never made it back.

Life for the messengers was a mixed bag. The messengers were positioned in various departments around the site and looked after the staff requirements on each floor of the main offices. They ran messages down the street, did post deliveries and generally were at the beck and call of the staff. The work could be quite boring but, on the other hand, we were able to read or study as much as we liked and were paid well enough that we could enjoy life to the full. It was the policy of the Brewery to encourage us to study, and huge pressure was applied on the boys to attend night school to obtain the Leaving Certificate. The Brewery paid the fees for night school and gave a sum of money for every exam passed.

The messengers in groups tended to work, play and socialise together. In 1954, the messengers' soccer team won the La Touche Cup with the youngest team ever to have played in the competition. The La Touche Cup was one of the best known and best attended sports events in Dublin; Iveagh Grounds, the Guinness sports complex in Crumlin, was always full to capacity for the final.

At that time, most of the senior managers started at ten in the morning and were gone by four. Between four and five in the afternoons, we played push ha'penny on the polished desks in the various offices around the Brewery. The push ha'penny 'championships' were usually held for money, with the contestants contributing to the kitty and the winner taking it all. These championships were banned by the men messengers who were in charge of the boys, mainly because of the damage that was done to the beautifully polished desks. Every so often, they would raid the offices, usually at a key point in a final, and we would all be up on a charge.

Initially, I was based in the post office and had to deliver the post all over the site. One particular run involved going out to Thomas Street and James's Street, then around by the Hop Store and the Malt House and back around to the Watling Street area. This meant going out on the street in my uniform, with my little pillbox cap – which I was supposed to wear – stuffed into the post bag so that it would not be seen. God, how I hated that post run! I felt so stupid wearing that hat: I dreaded being seen outside the Brewery by anyone I knew. Thankfully, I was soon transferred out of the post office to become directors' messenger.

When I was directors' messenger, the head messenger, in charge of all the messengers on site, was Jim Daly. The men messengers wielded great power over the boys and could, by writing up a bad report, do tremendous damage to their prospects of being kept on at eighteen. Jim, who was in his late fifties or early sixties at that time, had a great regard for the British. Being a Christian Brothers' boy, I had some difficulty in conversations with him when he would tell me that 'When the British were here the weather was great'!

In my time as directors' messenger, I worked for Sir Charles Harvey, who was the managing director at that time, as well as with Sir Richard Levinge and C. K. Mill. Sir Charles was very kind to me during my time as directors' messenger and always took an interest in what I was studying and how I was doing. He was one of the more progressive directors in Guinness: he negotiated with the union when the union first came into the company. His name continues to be honoured in the Irish Management Institute by the Sir Charles Harvey Award, which is presented every year.

In those days, the managing director lived in 98 James's Street, beside the power station. Sir Charles lived there with Lady Harvey and their two children, Marjorie and Charles Junior. It was a big house, with all the trappings of the television series *Upstairs Downstairs*.

During the summer, from four to six PM, Sir Charles held social functions for the brewery staff in his house at 98 James's Street – '98', as it was called. Invitations were sent to selected male and female staff to attend the functions on a nominated day. As directors' messenger, I was asked by Sir Charles to open the door and take the coats of the invited staff. For this I received ten shillings – a lot of money in those days, given that my weekly wage was two pounds. In addition, I got the opportunity to see Marjorie, Sir Charles's daughter, who was tall and thin, and with whom I was head over heels in love. At about 4.15 PM, she would bring me a plate of biscuits and a glass of milk. In my excitement, I could barely hold the tray; often, I spilt milk all over it – much to my embarrassment. At 4.20 PM, I was discharged, so I never got the chance to see what went on after that. Years later, when I was personnel director, I worked with Victor Leeson, of Guinness Choir fame. Victor often talked about those dreadful evenings when 'one was called upon to entertain the young ladies of the Brewery and was then thrown out on the street at six o'clock in broad daylight, with an obligation to take some young lady downtown to tea.'

One of my recollections of that time is of sitting beside Sir Charles in the boardroom while he read from a large manual. My job was to turn the page when he came to the end of a page, in much the same way as a pianist has someone to turn the pages of a score for him while he is playing. I sat on a stool and developed a technique of knowing when it was time to turn the page by noting the twitching of his knee. This was my first lesson in observing body language!

Before I left the Brewery, I became friendly with an American consultant, Josh Leibner, who was working with the Guinness organisation. He asked me if I had ever heard of Sir

Charles Harvey. In London, he had met Charles Junior, his son, who told him about his father managing the Guinness brewery. Through my friend, I invited Charles Junior to stay at 98 James's Street, his old family home, which was now being used to entertain overseas visitors. He came for a weekend with his sister Marjorie and their grown-up children, who were then in their twenties. The children had no practical experience of what life had been like for their parents in Dublin but had heard, over the years, of the life that their parents and grandparents had enjoyed.

At a dinner in 98 James's Street, Marjorie and Charles recalled how their father would leave for work around ten o'clock, have lunch at around half twelve and finish work around four o'clock. Sometimes, he would call over for a rest at lunchtime, and often when he got up at three 'there was little point in going back to work', as he put it, so he and his children would head off fishing or shooting. Although I would have seen Sir Charles as hard-working, many of the managers came to Guinness after serving in the Empire and saw their commission in Dublin as just reward for their efforts. Some of them did little more than sit in front of the fire and read the paper, rarely getting involved in any serious problems involving the company. I can speak authoritatively on this subject as I was one of those who lit the fire, left out their pens and newspapers, and watched the life and times they had in the company. One manager had his slippers laid out for him every morning!

I don't think I watched with envy because, having had a good Christian Brothers education and a Catholic upbringing, I had few expectations and knew my place in life. Still, at the time I spoke to Sir Charles's children about this, I was working sixty or seventy hours a week as managing director. I obviously switched to the management side of things too late!

During our messenger days in the Brewery, all of us teenagers became conscious of the opposite sex. We viewed the 'Lady Women', as the female clerical staff were known by us, with great interest. Indeed some of them, although viewed from afar, became the centre of our daily lives.

There was one such woman, Pat Connolly, who worked in the cask office on the top floor of the offices in James's Street. She was absolutely beautiful, nearly six feet tall, blonde, and an occasion of sin for every young boy in the office block. The cask-office ladies were entitled to two breaks a day because their offices were up in the attic; everyone else got only one break. They had a fifteen-minute break in the morning and in the afternoon, and in the summer would take their breaks in the front yard, sitting on seats that had been specially laid out for them.

One of the cask messengers' tasks was to send a signal throughout the whole office block when the cask girls were leaving to come down to sit in the sun – and to tell us when Pat Connolly was on the move. Every messenger who was based in the front office block was phoned, and they would then find some reason to pass along the corridor to try to catch a glimpse of this tall, blonde vision.

The whole idea of this scruffy crowd of boys having the cheek to peer around corners to ogle this fine specimen of a woman beggars belief, particularly given the fact that all of the boys were called by their surnames. Nonetheless, although most of us never even heard her speak, Pat Connolly brightened our lives during that difficult transition from boyhood to manhood.

The calling of employees by their surnames was reminiscent of the army and typified the autocratic structures that prevailed in the company. Even men messengers of a 'mature age' were called by their surnames by young women who had just joined the company!

On one occasion, I can remember standing with Jim Daly – Mr Daly, as we addressed him – when a number of young girls passed on their break. One new girl called out 'Hello Mr Daly' as she passed. He then turned to me and said: 'That little girl lives near us. You can see the difference good breeding makes.' The same girl passed a few days later and called out 'Good morning Daly' to him. In a very short time, she had learned how the Guinness hierarchy operated.

While working as a messenger, I was also studying for my Leaving Certificate. I attended Caffrey's College on Stephen's

Green, three nights a week. These nights developed into social sessions, as Caffrey's College was above an ice-cream–coffee parlour called the Green Lounge, to which we adjourned during our break at 8.30. The more studious students returned for the last session, from nine to ten, but the rest of us managed to escape; we usually headed for the Palm Grove ice-cream parlour in O'Connell Street. At the end of the year, I sat the Leaving. I achieved what was necessary for me to keep the pressure off both at home and in the Brewery – but only just.

Around this time, I was looking at what I might do in the future. I had my eyes on Scotland Yard, which was then undertaking a massive recruitment campaign. Part of the attraction of going to London to join Scotland Yard was that it involved two years' training in Bermuda. While I was studying for the Leaving, I usually walked home with a chap called Paddy Lawless, who lived beside me and was on the same course. He was extremely critical of my proposal to leave Ireland. He used to tell me how beautiful Dublin was, and how it was only fifteen minutes to either the sea or the mountains. He was so convincing that I tore up my pass to travel over for the interview. Six months later, I heard that he had emigrated!

For years, I gave out about Paddy Lawless and the fact that he went on to ignore his own advice. Some years ago, I was lecturing in Galway University when a lecturer came up to me and said 'Do you remember me? We went to night school together: my name is Paddy Lawless.' I left him in no doubt as to what I thought of him and how he had affected my life.


When boys were recruited into Guinness, there were two streams: messengers and laboratory attendants. Those who did very well in the exam went to the laboratories and were seen as the cream, while the messenger boys were seen as the lesser class.

At eighteen, messengers usually became number takers, until the age of twenty-one. As the name suggests, the number takers recorded the number of barrels going out into the trade. When

I reached eighteen, I passed the number-taking exam, but there were no vacancies in the department. To my horror, I was sent to the racking shed in the Traffic Department, the area where the kegs were filled with beer. My job was to paint the rim of the casks with the relevant identification colour, depending on the contents – a job known as raddling. A barrel of porter was given a white border, a brown border signalled stout, and a blue colour indicated that the cask was for export.

This was an extremely physically demanding job involving a great deal of bending down: it was hard on the poor back. I was often bent over, on and off, in this position from 6 AM until 3 PM, or even longer. It was tough going, but given that my football career was about to take off at the time, the bending down was good exercise for me as a goalkeeper. If nothing else, it was good practice for picking the ball out of the back of the net!

During my time in the racking shed, I worked with people who had a tremendous capacity to put away drink. Often the first task of the day in the racking shed, on the 6 AM shift, was for individuals to place the hose that would normally fill the barrels, into their mouths, pull the handle and give themselves their first fix of the day. These guys had no problem in participating in sports in their spare time, despite having consumed a significant number of pints during their shift.

When I arrived at the racking shed, my father was the supervisor there. This initially made me unpopular, and I had a difficult time there until I was finally accepted. The day I arrived, a Kerryman – who spoke a language I did not know – lifted me by the throat two feet off the ground and threatened that, if I ever told my father anything that went on there, he would break my f–ing neck. He then proceeded to drop me from a height. I didn't doubt him. When the same man retired from the Brewery thirty years later, he came all the way up to my office, which was situated on the upper level, to say goodbye and to apologise for attacking me that day.

The racking shed was not a pleasant place to work, and the long hours and conditions did nothing to improve my disposition. Nonetheless, my experiences of working there probably hardened me for my later career in the Brewery.

After some months, a vacancy arose in the number-takers', and I was duly transferred. I spent the next few years in idyllic contentment, wearing my civvies rather than the smocks and clogs of the racking shed. I enjoyed the work, taking note of the number of barrels being loaded into railway wagons for transportation all over Ireland. The figures were then supplied to the cask office, where there was a huge force of clerical staff, including the beautiful Pat Connolly, keeping track of where every cask was on any given day.

I had a very easy time of it and earned plenty of overtime, often working until one or two in the morning. In addition, we received a pound a month for correctly recording the numbers that were passed on to the cask office: we were allowed ten mistakes in a month. I don't know how they identified mistakes, but the extra pound that most of us got at the end of the month was more than welcome.

Years later, number taking was discontinued in the Brewery. Someone had obviously woken up to the fact that the actual cost of lost casks (known as 'out of control' casks) was significantly less than the cost of keeping the records. The cask office and the number takers' were closed down – with significant savings to the company.

Around this time, my football career began to take off. The Brewery reduced the working week to five days, Monday to Friday. (Before that, everyone had worked Saturday mornings as well.) Coincidentally, the week this new arrangement came into force, I signed on the dotted line for Holyhead Town in the North Wales League. The reduction in the working week allowed me to catch the mailboat from Dun Laoghaire to Holyhead on Friday night, travel to play wherever the match was in Wales, and then return on the 3.20 AM boat on Sunday morning.

At the age of twenty-one, my number-taking days finished; suddenly, I was a 'man', doing labouring work. On my first day out working as a 'man', I was given a boiler suit and safety shoes.

Then, the 'kinetic handling' expert was used to demonstrate how best to lift a full barrel with a straight back and knees bent. We lifted a full barrel together, one holding each end, and then proceeded to let it down onto the ground. Unfortunately, the instructor forgot to tell me to let go, and the barrel came down and split my fingers.

I was taken straightaway to the Medical Department, where I had my fingers bandaged up and was assigned light work for three weeks by the doctor. The embarrassment of having to return to my father, the supervisor, with a light work docket, only thirty minutes after becoming a 'man', was something I had trouble living with in the Guinness community for some time. Being a 'man' and competing with the strong country lads who seemed to have endless energy and strength was not easy – as I was about to find out.

While many people nostalgically look back on the old days, for others life in Guinness was very tough, with hard labouring work and long hours, often in terrible working conditions. The Guinness benefits package, including as it did the use of a free medical department, subsidised meals and other benefits, was streets ahead of that offered by other companies. The basic wage was low, however, and take home pay generally had to be supplemented by long hours of overtime.

At a union meeting in the Metropolitan Hall on one occasion, a union member took to the platform to argue forcefully that 'Now is the time for brewery men to get the wage everyone outside believes they have.' He went on to propose that, instead of looking for a rise of ten shillings per week, the union should look for a basic rate of £17 a week. There were gasps from the hall, as the basic rate at that time was £12; within two years, it had risen to £20.

People talk about the good old days, but they weren't so good for most. Men worked long hours, doing heavy physical work to earn extra money to bring up their wages. Conditions in many departments were atrocious. Visits to the toilet, which were pre-programmed at the start of the day, were recorded and timed by an attendant, known as a 'jacks clerk'. This person would issue each client with two pieces of toilet paper in return for the employee's pay disc, which he held until the employee had completed his 'business'.

In one particular case, a man needing to go to the toilet before his allotted toilet break was refused permission to do so. At the time, he was working on the top of the pile of wooden kegs outside the offices in the Cooperage. In full view of the 'ladies and gentlemen' of the Staff, he proceeded to drop his trousers – to roars from the foreman to come down immediately. The arrangements for toilet breaks were never applied so rigidly again!

Between 1959 and 1967, I worked in some of the worst jobs in the Brewery. The 'scald bank' area in the cooperage was the dirtiest, and the steamiest. In this area, wooden casks came back from the trade and were opened to make sure that they contained no foreign bodies or contamination. The fact that there was always steam and rotten beer all over the floor made it a dreadful place to work. One of tasks done in the area was to lift the casks up to the cooper's nose for him to smell them. (The coopers were such an elite group in the Brewery that they wouldn't even bend down on a rail to smell a cask – not one inch.) If the cask smelt 'sweet', it was okay to use; if it was 'sour', it had to go for special treatment.

An opportunity arose to transfer to the Traffic Department, where everyone wanted to work, and I and five others transferred. On transfer, I worked in the garage. It was tough going: as well as our ordinary 8 AM to 5 PM days, three days a week we worked until ten at night, refuelling and cleaning the fleet of two hundred lorries and the directors' cars. When a job assessment was done for all the jobs in the Brewery, the six of us working in the garage were graded at the lowest level on the entire site.

The supervisor in the garage area ruled with an iron fist: we were never allowed to move out of the garage into the rest of the Brewery, even for ten minutes. I thoroughly resented the controls that were put on me there and was in constant trouble with this supervisor. So bad was our relationship that on one occasion, when the supervisor asked me to wash the managing director's car, which was in the garage to have a problem with the door repaired, he shouted after me: 'And for f–'s sake don't tell me you weren't told there was a door missing.' He was afraid I would ruin the inside of the car by spraying the whole thing regardless – and he was probably right!

My work in the garage was completely menial. On one occasion, one of the mechanics put it to me that my father must be ashamed of me, working in this job, given his position in the company. This was a real dig at me: I began to realise that it must have been difficult for him to see his own son in this job and not to be able to do anything about it. He could not be seen to show favouritism.

*

What kept me sane was the life I lived outside the Brewery, playing soccer. At that time, I was playing for Morton in Scotland, having been bought from Shelbourne, and I had a tight schedule at the weekends, travelling to Glasgow every Friday evening. My father drove me in his Volkswagon to the airport. I had a huge fear of flying, and I always made sure that I went to Confession before I left. If I was going to die, I at least knew that I would be 'going up'.

My father and I would leave the Brewery about five o'clock and he would park outside John's Lane Church. I would run into the church and into the confession box. Then, barely on one knee, I would say quickly what I had to confess, while my father sat in the car with the engine running. It all had to be done with split-second timing, as the flight left at 7 PM and there was no question of getting off work early to play football. In the early days of my time commuting to Scotland, we always flew on a Saturday. One week we got snowed in in Dublin, however, so we didn't risk it after that.

I remember one Friday when things didn't go to plan. We went through the usual routine: we pulled up outside church, then I ran in, knelt down, said my piece and started to get up to go. But before giving absolution, the priest asked me where I thought I was going. Without realising what he meant, I replied: 'Scotland.'

'You're going nowhere without absolution,' he said slowly, clearly and very definitely. 'Have you told these sins before?'

'Every week,' I proudly replied. I don't know what I was thinking. Perhaps I thought I was so good merely to be going to Confession every week, or perhaps I felt that I was keeping him in business. Whatever my motivation, this was not the right answer for this particular priest on this particular day.

'There's no purpose of amendment here, so there's no absolution.' He was adamant.

I put my other knee to the floor of the confession box and went into a state of mild shock. There was no way I was stepping onto an aeroplane without absolution; but he was right, it was likely that my usual minor sins would be committed again – something that had never before occurred to me.

I could picture the plane coming down, with my soul committed to burn in hell forever. I really believed that at the time. This was the worst situation I had had to deal with in a long time. After a minute or two, I pulled myself together and, using the best of my negotiating skills, persuaded the priest to give me absolution. He agreed, provided that I agreed to return to him after the match in Scotland. I ran out and just about made the flight. Of course, I chose carefully who I went to for Confession after that, and I never went back to that priest again.

\*

In 1967, the manager of the Traffic Department decided to create four promotional opportunities for people to move from the shop floor to the staff. It is difficult to explain the enormity of this decision, given the horizons it would open up for people who had expected to be doing labouring work until they reached the retirement age of sixty-five.

Practically everyone who was eligible applied for promotion. Following several interviews, the numbers were eventually whittled down to eight people, who were to be interviewed by the head of personnel and the head of the Traffic Department.

I was one of the lucky ones to get through to the final eight. Given my father's position, most people seemed to think that I was home and dry. However, on the morning of the interviews, which were held in the visitors' centre at the top of Watling Street, as I walked up the hill I met a union shop steward, Jim Marsh, who had just been interviewed. He told me: 'You're f–ed. You have no chance.' When I asked him what he meant, all he would say was that I would find out for myself.

As I took my seat in front of the two gentlemen who were to interview me, I very quickly found out what Jim Marsh had meant. One of the interviewers announced that 'These positions are to be filled regardless of who people are.' This signalled to me quite clearly that they were determined to prove that they were honest and that the appointment process was transparent. I knew then that I would not be one of the successful candidates, but I still hoped that I would be. When the results came out, I was gutted to find out that I had not been successful. It felt like the end of the world. I sat in our house, feeling numb, with my wife and my parents. My father was even more devastated. It was unlikely that such an opportunity would come again.

At this time, my football career had come to an end due to injury and so this diversion was no longer available to me. Anyway, football had become a drudge to me: training and travelling had taken their toll, and I had gone soft. I had no desire to go out on cold winter nights to train and play matches. I had become the victim of a cosy life.

My chance of advancement in Guinness seemed to be gone, and I felt doomed to face a long life of labouring work. A few months later, however, out of the blue, one of the clerks in the despatch office of the Traffic Department decided to emigrate to Australia. Miraculously – maybe due to my mother's prayers – I was appointed to this position. This was my second stroke of good luck in Guinness. It was an unbelievable breakthrough for me. To quote the manager at the time, Mr Boucher: 'You have made the big breakthrough in life and will now have a totally different lifestyle.'

The man who spoke to me on my appointment was one of the two who had interviewed – and rejected – me a few months previously. Such was the snobbery that existed in the Brewery at the time, this manager asked me whether I thought my wife would be able to keep up with the new social environment I was going to be mixing in! He also told me that, while I had done very well to break out of a weekly paid labouring job to the clerical position, this would be my job until I retired at sixty-five. He stressed that I would have no chance of being promoted further. As he seemed to believe that I had already made the big time and was set up for life, this was of no consequence, in his view.

This man spent half an hour talking to me about his ships, his lorries, his railway wagons and his men. He would have been excellent government-minister material, given that they always seem to talk about *their* budget and *their* money, as if these things were their own.

After my promotion, I had to go to the chief medical officer for a medical examination before being appointed to the staff. This was despite the fact that I was already an employee and had attended the Guinness Medical Department regularly for fifteen years.

The Medical Department was based in a big house at the back of the Brewery. It had two entrances: the front entrance was used by staff, and the back entrance was used by workers, who were paid weekly – like a tradesman's entrance in a 'big house'. Needless to say, I knew my place and went around to the back entrance. I took my card and waited to be called. At the end of the examination, as I was leaving, I headed for the back entrance again but was told sharply by the doctor to go through the front entrance, as I was now 'staff'. In the space of fifteen minutes, I had made the progression from being part of the masses to one of a select group.

I was twenty-nine at the time, and was married, with one child and another on the way. My salary was now £1,000 per year

– a jump from £800. In 1963, I had bought my house for £2,300. The promotion meant that I had money and status and did not have to worry about making mortgage repayments. Just as importantly for me, I had escaped my mundane job in the garage.

Being 'staff', I also had the power to write scrips (chits) for pints for individuals or groups. There were drinking facilities all around the brewery, known as 'taps'. Employees would go to these to drink their allowance during the course of their working shifts. Given that the Brewery taps operated from 5 AM until possibly 2 AM the following morning, they were in constant use. Many individuals, in addition to their normal allowance of two pints a day, could accumulate anything up to an additional fifteen or twenty pints by doing extra work for their foreman or by obtaining scrips from their workmates who might not take a drink.

On one of my first nights as a clerk, while I was doing my lock-up rounds at 2 AM, I spotted that one of these taps, which should have been closed at least a couple of hours previously, was open. As I approached the back door, it was obvious that a party was in full swing. I could hear an accordion and fiddle being played and several people singing. It was a difficult situation for me to be in. Having just come from the shop floor, I wasn't at all comfortable with the idea of spoiling anyone's fun – and being given abuse for doing so.

I gave the back door of the tap a few hefty bangs, hoping that this would serve as a warning that a clerk was coming. I somewhat foolishly hoped that everyone might take flight, or at least that the party would cool down a bit. Instead, I was greeted instead with a roar that the door was locked, in case the bloody so-and-so clerk came by. The revellers proceeded to tell me to come on around to the front and they would let me in.

This was my first introduction to making difficult management decisions. I went around to the front and told them all to go off home – that I would go and do the rest of the round and that I didn't want to find them there when I came back. When I got back, luckily for all of us they had disappeared and the place was locked up, as it should have been before. Another crisis averted!

A colleague who was working on a similar shift was not so lucky. After doing his rounds, he locked up the racking-shed area at 2 AM and then went to sleep until 5 AM as usual, in the James's Street house provided by the company. When he came to open the racking-shed door at 6 AM, he nearly had a heart attack when a dishevelled figure fell out of the shed on top of him. This man had been locked in by mistake and had obviously amused himself by drinking heavily all night

Another area of responsibility for me as a member of staff was to ensure the enforcement of the Brewery's rigid no-smoking policy. This was also sure to make me unpopular because to be caught smoking meant an instant fine of a quarter of a week's wages. One particular story told was of a clerk who entered the changing rooms on an inspection. Only one guy was there, and he had his foot up on the bench, pulling on his protective shoes. There on the bench next to him was a smouldering cigarette. The clerk stood glaring down at the man while he, cool as a cucumber, continued putting on his shoes. Eventually, as the cigarette was just about to burn through the bench, the clerk roared" 'Who owns that cigarette?' The man coolly responded: 'I don't know, but I don't think he'll be coming back for it.'

At that time, 'pillaging' (robbing beer) was a dismissal offence. Of course it went on nevertheless. Men bored holes in beer pipes and placed pegs in them. When the coast was clear, they would take out the peg and fill their cans, mugs and bottles with beer.

My first few months as a junior manager were mostly spent in the traffic-control office, setting up a new cost-control system for the transport section. This was the area which planned the routes for all the lorries throughout Ireland. At that time, beer was distributed in tank to nearly seventy bottlers around the country, who bottled the Guinness and then sold it themselves. In later years, the Brewery discontinued this practice for quality-control purposes. At the time, there was a huge distribution fleet, with more than two hundred drivers employed. The Road Transport Department also collected grain from all the maltings around the country – places such as Wexford, Enniscorthy and Durrow – where barley was malted specially for Guinness.

In addition, we had about forty lorries delivering to pubs in the Dublin area. Traffic control was an exciting office to work in: it was all action and crisis and was often referred to as 'bomber command'. Some drivers also jokingly said that the planning results often resembled the results of a bombing mission: chaos and confusion.

After a number of months in the traffic-control office, I was asked to go to work with Freddie Byrne, the accountant for the Traffic Department. The prospect of this filled me with horror, as Freddie always seemed to me to be very grumpy. The thought of working in a quiet office with him filled me with dread, especially after I had enjoyed all the hustle and bustle of traffic control.

This move was the initiative of Jim Bradshaw, who was personnel manager in the Traffic Department and was also the spotter of talent for Harry Hannon, the manager of the department. Jim was also a great mentor and developer of people he believed had the ability to progress in the Brewery. He coached me through my early days as a member of staff and was my mentor for many years. This was particularly generous of him, because he and my father did not get on at all.

Despite my initial misgivings, the three years I spent working for Freddie Byrne turned out to be my most productive years in the Brewery, certainly as far as learning was concerned. Freddie was a genius with figures: he wasn't just an accountant, he could make figures talk. I had always had a love of figures myself, and I threw myself into this new role with great enthusiasm.

Freddie could produce figures for the manager that would show whatever he, Freddie, wanted – that a particular section was, or was not, performing well. Depending on where he started the review, he could show anything he wanted to! He met with the Traffic Department manager every Friday; if someone had annoyed him during the week, he would take great pleasure in painting a less-than-flattering picture of their particular section. This would result in a phone call from the head of the department, telling the relevant manager to come to his office immediately.

Freddie was one of the most interesting people I worked with. He had a tremendous grasp of a wide range of topics and was extremely knowledgeable. Above all, he had a fantastic sense of humour, and we spent a lot of time laughing and joking. Mondays were the exception to this rule. Freddie liked to go for a few drinks on Sunday night. As a result, on Monday mornings he could be grumpy; in fact, he used to say very little until at least lunchtime. He was often in a philosophical mood, and it was then that he discussed in detail whether or not God existed and whether there was such a thing as 'the hereafter'. Most Mondays, he did believe, but occasionally he made the point that, if there was nothing in the hereafter, and we all just turned into black pudding, we'd all have wasted time living good lives.

After three years working with Freddie, I was promoted to take charge of the traffic-control office to replace Christy Hayes, the Dublin hurler, who was transferring to C&C, one of the companies in the Guinness Group. This caused resentment among other members of staff because I had been promoted to staff only a short while before. More contentious was the fact that two men who were my father's contemporaries worked in the office. The climate was not good for a while, but I eventually gained their support and over the years they became amongst my closest friends. The atmosphere in the traffic-control office was tremendous, with great camaraderie and hilarity even at times of crisis.

Shortly after being appointed to my first management post, in charge of the road-transport operation, I was suddenly confronted with the reality of responsibility. Within the space of two months, our lorry fleet was involved in three major accidents, two of them with fatal consequences for the occupants of the other vehicles involved.

Being called out on a winter's night to the scene of a tragic accident and having to take control on behalf of the company brought home to me the fact that I had moved into a new period in my life. From that moment on, I was very conscious of the obligations that came with responsibility.

Adapting to being on the Staff did not initially come easily to me. One of our tasks as clerks in the control office was to check the driver log sheets to ensure that the claims made for payment were legitimate. Dealing with men who were older than myself, sometimes my father's age, was difficult, not because of anything they did but because of my respect for age.

When disciplining people, on the few occasions it was necessary, I was always conscious that the person sitting opposite me was king in his own house, and looked up to by family and friends. Having known all the drivers for the whole of my working life, managing them caused tensions on a few occasions in the early stages. Indeed, when I queried one driver, who had been a messenger with me, about his log-sheet returns, he angrily retorted: 'Your father was a gentleman.' That left me in no doubt where I stood!

These encounters also brought their lighter moments. I once confronted one driver who had claimed half an hour extra overtime because his lorry was 'not pulling properly going up Howth Head'. I called him in and we had an argument over his claim. I took great pleasure in eventually disallowing the payment, claiming that he had the benefit of going downhill on the far side of Howth Head! In my innocence, I was delighted with myself: this was my first management success. The next day, however, my colleague Mick Cullen, who had been on late duty checking log-sheets called me over to view the driver's log-sheet for that day. Written across the sheet was 'claiming half hour for time spent discussing previous day's sheet with Mr Flood'!

During the winter, we could have lorries stranded all over the country due to snow on the roads and other extreme weather conditions. We could have a lorry in January buried for days in the snow in the Barnesmore Gap in Donegal, which always seemed to become impassable due to snow in the wintertime. The drivers were in charge of big lorries full of tanks of beer, and they had to work in frost and snow, leaving at six in the morning to travel from Dublin to places as far apart as Kerry or Donegal. My job was to oversee the rostering of the fleet of vehicles to ensure that the bottlers got the beer they needed, when they needed it. Job satisfaction came daily – as did problems. For one thing, we had major problems with access to pubs in Dublin, which didn't open before 10 AM and didn't want deliveries at lunchtime. Moreover, in most parts of Dublin, by-laws meant that deliveries had to be complete before 5 PM.

One of the strange customs in relation to Guinness staff was that, in the dining room, established staff had their own individual places at certain tables. New staff members had to stand in a line at the back of the dining room and wait for the head waiter, Mr Melia, to place them at a table. It wasn't unusual to be placed at a table of six, where the other five would not talk to you at all and would just continue their conversation around you. On the other hand, when I eventually got a placing at a table, as I became better established among the staff, I had no problems and was made to feel extremely welcome by all at the table. A lot depended on the particular individuals.

One of my colleagues on the 'unclassified staff' went to dinner in the dining room at seven o'clock, on the evening shift, and sat at the only table that was set for dinner. There was only a handful of people working late in the Brewery at that time, and an engineer was the only other person seated at the same table. The engineer completely ignored this man during the meal, and they both ate in silence. Such was the line between those who were anointed and those who were appointed, from the shop floor.

During my time in charge of the traffic-control office, I was asked by my boss to travel to Deasy's, a drinks-distribution company in Cork that was a subsidiary of Guinness, to undertake a survey of their distribution system and to put forward proposals for reductions in their fleet. I was warned beforehand that I was unlikely to get a warm reception from the management team there. When I arrived, however, relationships were even more difficult than I had thought possible. The management team certainly did not want anyone from Dublin being imposed on them. In fact, they ignored me completely. The drivers were all football fanatics and big Cork Celtic fans, however, so *we* at least had no difficulties in relating to each other.

After three weeks compiling my survey – during which time I travelled on the lorries and played darts in various pubs, among other things – I had to face the fact that my proposals were likely to lead to a reduction in the size of the fleet. Given the relationship that I had built up with the drivers, I dreaded having to do what had to be done there. However, we had a chat in a pub during their keg deliveries and reached an understanding, before the proposals were drawn up!

After a number of years in charge of the control office, I was appointed manager of the Road Transport Department. My overall responsibilities didn't change much, but I gained a fancier title and a higher grade, and was paid a bigger salary.

At about this time, we were recovering from a strike that had hit Guinness in 1974 – the first one in the more than two-hundred-year history of the Brewery.

The strike became a landmark in the company's history. It highlighted the fact that the divisions and social barriers across the Brewery made it more difficult for problems to be resolved, as people did not talk to each other across the barriers. As a result, the company set up the Brewery Council to try to integrate the various groups. Around 1977, my boss, Harry Hannon, told me that the managing director, Paddy Galvin, and the head of personnel, Brian Walsh, wanted me to move to the personnel section. This was shortly after I had produced a paper outlining where I thought the company was going wrong and what should be done to improve relationships within it. I had written this paper in anger for Harry Hannon while I was watching how the company was being run – with no leadership, no direction, and no strategy. I thought the paper had gone nowhere, but years later, when I became personnel director, I found it, filed away with the comments my then colleagues had made about it at the time. The paper obviously caught the eye of Brian Walsh and Paddy Galvin, who brought me to the Personnel Department.

I was absolutely delighted when they outlined the job speci-fication for the post I was being offered. If I had been asked to write my own job specification, I couldn't have written a better one. It was everything I wanted in a job. It was a job that gave me the freedom to get involved in personnel issues at all levels of the company.

At that time, however, I was a member of the graded staff – an integrated system of all junior- and middle-management staff across the company. The next stage up was a senior-management post – which meant you were really going places. My boss, Harry Hannon, had understood that my new post in personnel would be at the next stage, i.e. senior management, but when I went to talk to Paddy Galvin and Brian Walsh, there was no men-tion of this. On my return to the Traffic Department, there was an urgent summons from Harry. The first thing he said to me was: 'I hope you didn't mention the bit about it being a senior-management post' – to which I replied that I hadn't. 'Good,' he said, 'because it's not available, it's not on offer.' I had to wait for another couple of years before I got my senior-management grade.

The Personnel Department was not what I had expected. Having come from the transport section, which was mainly task-orientated and where the time span for achievement was relative-ly short, I arrived into an area where nothing ever seemed to fin-ish. This was difficult for me to accept. I began to feel that, because the issues being dealt with were likely to occur over and over again, if I came back ten years later, I would be dealing with the same issues with different names. Moreover, most of the projects in the Personnel Department required an inordinate amount of preparation, discussion and negotiation before they got anywhere near the stage of being implemented.

I was on the verge of seeking a transfer from personnel when an older colleague explained to me that this department was a bit like the guy on the stage with the plates twirling around on sticks. The trick was to keep the sticks turning while making sure that the plates never come crashing down. If one did come crashing down, another could replace it, and the show could go on. It was all about keeping things moving and making key interventions at the right moment – when the stick wobbled, as it were. The timing of such interventions was the real secret to success, he told me. I took notice of this piece of advice and decided to stick things out.

Eventually, I settled into personnel and actually began to enjoy the work, particularly the industrial-relations side of things, which was the key part of the work of the department. Personnel functions were male-dominated and confrontational, with a lot of head-bangers – including myself, it has to be said – shouting at each other day after day. Personnel conferences and training courses, for instance, were dominated by men, with only a few women present. Now, of course, the reverse is the norm, with industrial relations way down the pecking order of competencies required by a well-qualified personnel executive.

Working on my own in silence, in a quiet office, was also a whole new experience for me. The silence didn't agree with my temperament, and I would open the door to the main office in the hope of hearing voices and noise. It was also the first time I had the benefits of a secretarial service. I initially found the simple task of making contact with her through the intercom embarrassing and would instead open the door and say 'Can you come in?' I wasn't comfortable asking someone to do something for me and was very deferential to my secretary to begin with – which probably made her uncomfortable.

People problems dominated the 1980s for Guinness. There was a lot of aggro around because of the constant change programmes. Many managers did not want to get into a confrontational situation with employees on any issue, with the result that appeasement was the order of the day. I prospered in this environment. I loved the negotiations, the cut and thrust, the planning, and the implementation of strategies for change. In a very short space of time, my amount of influence had greatly outpaced my position in the company. I was at the centre of all the action, with Paddy Galvin and Brian Walsh, and subsequently with Brian Patterson and Clive Brownlee. Within a couple of years, I was given free rein to deal with industrial-relations in the company. In my first performance appraisal, my boss, Brian Walsh, started by informing me that he had both good and bad news for me. Fearing the worst, I asked for the good news first, to which he replied: 'You are doing a great job. Everyone is saying they never saw anyone more suited to a job.' He went on to say: 'Unfortunately, that's also the bad news: you'll never be able to get away from the industrial-relations job.' This was my first lesson in career management: I quickly realised that it was essential to have a replacement for myself trained up speedily.

Around 1980, I began working with Brian Patterson. He was a workaholic, as well as being a real visionary and a man of great integrity. Over dinner one night on a business trip in London, we decided that we were going to attempt to change the culture of the company, particularly its management style, which at the time tended to be one of appeasement. We mapped out the future of the Brewery on table napkins, asking for more every half an hour or so! Prior to 1981, management tended to capitulate every time they came under pressure from the union. In 1981, we had discussions with the union until 2 AM in an effort to resolve a particular dispute. When the talks broke down, the shop stewards themselves expressed puzzlement as to how they had arrived at a strike situation. We on the management team found out that, during the day of our meeting, some of our colleagues in senior management had been telling the shop stewards that the company would capitulate. We had strikes in 1981 and in 1982: the former because of the appointment of a particular supervisor to a management post, and the latter because of a refusal on the part of the company to give two extra days' leave, which was an optional part of the national pay agreement that had come into force at that time. In 1983, we were heading for a hat-trick of strikes but, more by luck than judgement, we had a trouble-free year.

A few days into the 1981 strike, Des Byrne, then the personnel director, sent for Brian Patterson and myself and asked us how we proposed to settle the strike. We hadn't given this any thought, as we believed that right was on our side and that we should therefore stand firm. In our inexperience, we had given no thought to having an exit strategy. It only then dawned on us that even a strike has to be managed. This was a salutary lesson for us.

Over the next few years, the Personnel Department – led, initially, by Brian Patterson and myself, and then by Clive Brownlee and myself – worked to change the management style at the company. The department produced a booklet highlighting where the company should be in ten years' time – in 1994. This booklet then became our bible. It contained ten principles on which the company would operate, relating to management style, skills requirements, structure and organisation. The change in management style entailed a greater emphasis on leadership and the ability to manage change. This was necessary in order to deal with the changing environment in which the company found itself operating, with competition growing in the marketplace.

In the early 1980s, however, Paddy Galvin, then managing director, supported by Clive Brownlee, personnel director, and myself as personnel manager, put forward a paper to develop the Hop Store as a visitor centre. At the time, the marketing and sales people were totally against the idea, believing that it had no commercial value. After the Hop Store was opened as a visitor centre with the 1984 ROSC exhibition, all that changed.

The night the Hop Store opened was one of great pride for all of us. It was a balmy summer night, and ambassadors from many countries attended. That night, Brian Slowey, who had come in from C&C, very emotionally said to me: 'I now know what it means to be part of Guinness.'

One of the few light moments in the very stressful preparations during the day was when one of our colleagues, Ted Rowlette, was sent up to help the ROSC committee get control of a chaotic preparation situation. He gathered all the thirty to forty people working for ROSC together and threatened to sack them all if they didn't shape up. As he ranted, raved and threatened, someone whispered in his ear that they were all volunteers!

In 1980, after three years in Personnel, I was appointed personnel manager. By this stage, I had lost all feelings of inferiority and was immersed in the planning for the Future Competitiveness Plan with Paddy Galvin, then managing director, and Clive Brownlee, then personnel director. As part of the team, planning, negotiating and implementing FCP, life was hectic, with long hours, meeting after meeting, crisis after crisis. Our lives were dominated by the Plan.

After a few years as personnel manager, I required another challenge and felt I could take on more, such was the change in my level of confidence. I began to look outside the company and came very close to leaving to become personnel director of Braun in Carlow. My restlessness was known within the company, however, and in a restructuring I was given responsibility for the General Services Department, which had six hundred employees and covered catering, security and the upkeep of the sixty-acre site at St James's Gate.

Shortly after I took over the General Services Department, an explosion rocked the Brewery and surrounding areas. At 4.30 AM on the morning of Saturday 13 October 1986, there a massive explosion in the $CO_2$ plant which resulted in extensive damage to plant, equipment and buildings in the vicinity. The blast damaged many of the buildings at the back of the Brewery, and it was a miracle that no one was killed. Initially, there were fears that it had been a bomb, but it turned out that one of the $CO_2$ storage tanks had exploded. One of the cylindrical tuns had taken off like a rocket and landed in a backyard nearby – fortunately without injuring anyone.

We set up a system to enable people in the area to make claims for damage to property and possessions. Not surpisingly,

With my parents and sisters Kalleen (back) and Mary

My grandparents and Aunt Cathy (centre)

With Suzie, Ann and Barry

Kirwan Rovers, with Jimmy Lynch and
Maurice Fitzsimons

The confirmation class at Brunswick Street with Paddy Crosbie
The author is fourth from right in the front row

At Roscrea with my parents, Brother Finbarr and my sister Kalleen

'Keep your thoughts to yourself' – the usual advice
With my father at a Guinness pensioners' Christmas dinner

The Flood brothers
Josh and Alex

On the way to a football
match with Aunt Cathy

At my niece Eimear's wedding: from left, Anne, Suzie, Barry, Mary,
the author and Kalleen

My grandfather Dick Byrne, a Guinness drayman, and his horse Roy

Signing for Morton in the Gresham Hotel on 20 November 1961
From left: the author, Paddy Turner and Danny Traynor, the then
chairman of Shelbourne

At the Brewery with, from left,
Dick Spring, Glenys and Neil Kinnock
and, in the background, Ruairí Quinn

The lighter side of the job! With
models after a charity fashion show
at the Guinness Reception Centre

The tenth anniversary of the Brewery Council, 1987

The St John's Road
Guinness railway siding

With my wife Anne and my father on my retirement from Guinness in 1994

The railway loading bank, with number-takers
counting the casks

The Dublin board at work in the 1950s
Sir Charles Harvey is on the left

Guinness barges on the Liffey passing the Four Courts

Barley being spread along the floor after steeping

Making a presentation to the hundred-year-old widow of a
Brewery pensioner

As part of a government think-in at Barretstown Castle

Showing President Mary McAleese around Fatima Mansions

'Resting' with Roy Keane the day before Ireland's match against Italy in Giants Stadium, played on 18 June 1994

With Mick McCarthy

Shalbourne v. St Patrick's Athletic at Tolka Park, March 1961

Morton v. Celtic in the Scottish Cup, 27 January 1962
From left to right: Hughes (Celtic), Kiernan, Flood, Cowie (all Morton)

Playing in the 1960 Cup Final, with broken fingers on left hand strapped up

At Dalymount Park, 1961: note the size of the crowd!

Shamrock Rovers v. Shelbourne: punching clear from Paddy Ambrose

Shelbourne v. Cork Hibs in the 1960 FAI Cup Final

Shamrock Rovers minors, 1958

Shelbourne FC, FAI Cup winners, 1960
Back row: Doyle, Tony Dunne, Flood, Kelly, O'Brien, Strahan
Front row: Barber, Conroy, Theo Dunne, Wilson, Hennessy

Virginians, FAI Junior Cup winners, 1959

Morton FC, Renfrewshire Cup winners, 1961

perhaps, a big queue formed outside the front gate. The person dealing with the claims was reputed to have remarked that the local area must have had the highest concentration of Waterford glassware per capita in Ireland! As the explosion could have killed and maimed many people, we were generous when it came to the claims.

During my early days in Personnel, when I was trying to impress, I undertook to take the top union officials to Staveley in England to meet the British Steel shop stewards and managers that Brian Patterson and I had met six months earlier. My secretary organised all the air and rail tickets and our itinerary for the trip. When I came back from a late meeting one evening at seven o'clock, everything was laid out for me for the next morning, including my itinerary.

I followed the instructions. We arrived in Manchester, boarded the train to Oxenholme, changed at Oxenholme for Preston, and changed at Preston for Staveley. When we arrived in Staveley, as we were getting out of the train, the small guard at the end of the train remarked in his best British accent: 'I've never seen twelve people get out here before.' As we got out of the train carriage, I realised why. We were in a very rural setting. I immediately got a knot in my stomach. My unease was not helped by the presence of a cow, looking over a fence at us and moo-ing as we all passed by. When we got out of the station, we looked around: all we could see down in the village below us was about five houses and a pub, to which we adjourned immediately. When we walked in, I asked the man behind the bar where British Steel was. He replied: 'I don't know, mate. Where do you *think* it is?' When I said to him 'Staveley', he responded: 'Which of them? There are six Staveleys in England.'

The penny dropped, and I realised we were lost. I rang the office and asked pointedly: 'Which of the six Staveleys in England are we supposed to be in?' I heard an exclamation from my secretary and the phone went down. Eventually, having made contact again with someone in the office back home and having got the number for the company, I rang British Steel management and told them that the plane was delayed in Dublin and asked was there any chance they could come to Manchester to meet us at 6 PM. Initially, this caused a few problems, as it meant that the shop stewards would have to go home to their various locations. Eventually, however, they agreed to meet us in the hotel in Manchester. Boy was I relieved!

We then, of course, had the problem of getting ourselves back to Manchester. Although my colleagues were most reluctant to put down their pints, I managed to hustle them out of the pub. Back up the hill we went as the little train came back along the single track, with the guard looking out the door. When I explained to him that we needed to get back to Manchester by teatime – it was 2 PM at this stage – he told us that the train connections meant that we would not get there in time.

I immediately went around the village to see if there was anybody who would drive us part of the way. We spotted a bus outside the school. We offered the driver £30 to drive us half the way. He was most reluctant, saying that he had to take the schoolkids home. When I increased the offer to £60, he agreed to do it. He then went off to inform the kids that they would have to find their own way home. In the bus, as we travelled along, I realised that trying to get another train in Preston was going to be difficult, so I said that we'd give him £100 to get us back to the hotel before the British Steel people arrived – even though, at that stage, I didn't know where they were coming from.

He drove like mad along the motorway. Just as we were arriving at the hotel, at 6 PM, the British Steel shop stewards and managers were arriving. They thought we had come from the airport and were very sympathetic to our being delayed at Dublin Airport. We didn't bother to inform them that we had been on a tour of God-knows-where.

I subsequently discovered that the Staveley we had been in was in the Lake District, when, some months later, my colleague Victor Leeson sent me a postcard from the same village with a little note saying: 'Wish you were here. Oh no, you have been, haven't you!'

I would never have lived down the consequences of coming back to Dublin without meeting the union people we had gone to see in England. In fairness, none of the union people disclosed the story of the near-disaster when we got back, but one of my management colleagues did! One lesson I learned from this episode was that, no matter how bad the mistake you make, if you can recover from it, all is well. The power of recovery is everything.

Being appointed managing director of Guinness Dublin in 1989 was a tremendous honour and thrill for me, particularly as I had come into the company as a boy of fourteen in 1953. To be appointed managing director of the most famous brewery in the world at the age of fifty was, given the history of the company, a major breakthrough. It happened when my predecessor, Clive Brownlee, was appointed managing director of Guinness Nigeria.

The day after my appointment, Gay Byrne remarked on his radio programme how people in our two families who had gone before us would be delighted with the news. Within minutes, someone who obviously knew the Guinness set-up, phoned in and said that it was the equivalent of Ian Paisley being made pope! While this was over the top, my appointment nevertheless gave a lot of people a boost – particularly those people who had gone into the Brewery as boys and had worked for forty or fifty years in the company.

Becoming managing director should have been the highlight of my career. Strangely enough, though, the biggest thrill had come before that, in 1985, when I was made personnel director and joined the board of Guinness Dublin. For someone with my background – leaving school at fourteen and growing up in inner-city Dublin – to make the breakthrough to director was phenomenal.

When I was made personnel director, Brian Slowey had told me, over a cup of tea, how pleased he was about my appointment because he knew what the promotion would mean for my family, and my father in particular. Generations of our family had toiled in the Brewery, and now this!

Brian told me that his biggest regret was that, when *he* had made his mark in Guinness, his father wasn't around to see it. He said his father, who had been a publican in Francis Street, would really have enjoyed the fact that his son had made good within the Guinness empire.

When I became managing director, my first task, as I saw it, was to acquire a more comprehensive appreciation of all the functions in the company. As personnel director, I had at times been very critical of some of the other functions and thought that personnel, which had driven the change programmes over the years throughout the organisation, was the be-all and end-all. Evidence of the power of the personnel function was the fact that the two previous managing directors, Paddy Galvin and Clive Brownlee, had also been personnel director before being made managing director. This state of affairs is probably unique in any business.

Having sat around the board table and often been critical of various functions and directors, I now had to learn to respect each one and to see them as part of my team. I had to grasp that personnel was merely one part of a matrix of functions in Guinness.

In order to develop team spirit and to build our team skills, the board travelled to an adventure centre in Killary in Mayo that specialised in team training. Unfortunately, the personalities of the various individuals would not naturally allow the group to function as a team. The one lesson I learnt from our experiences in Killary was that the members of the Guinness board were unlikely ever to be a team that would die for each other. Nonetheless, we did have a good range of opinions, skills and personalities; they just needed to be harnessed to achieving a common purpose. I realised that I had to be conscious of the fact that I needed to tread warily in maximising each individual's contribution, in the interest of the group.

In one exercise in Killary, we were dropped off, all wrapped up in our boots and rainwear, on top of a mountain in the middle of a wet and windy night. As we drove along in the van before being dropped off, I began to think that we must be mad. Looking at my colleagues, I felt I was in the film *The Dirty Dozen*. We were given a compass and torch and, using various clues, were required to find twelve flags scattered over a large part of the mountain. One member of the group forcefully argued that he knew the direction to take and insisted that we go his way. A flag was to be at the ruin of a particular cottage on the mountain. When we arrived where this director had told us to go, he was perplexed to find that there was no flag. He hurled abuse into the night, believing that there were observers on the mountain watching what was going on. He was unaware that the flag was on another ruin close by, invisible in the dark, rainy night. Tempers ran so high throughout the night that at one stage some members of the group ended up threatening each other. So much for team spirit!

Another exercise had three of us travelling on mountain bikes for twenty miles to find hidden objects. By the time we got to our destination, our backsides were so sore that finding hidden clues was irrelevant to us: all we could think about was the skin we had lost from our nether regions. We found it difficult to cycle home – standing up. The next day, when the work was being allocated amongst the group, I drew the bikes again – much to my horror.

The team-building exercise on the mountain taught me never to be too far out in front of the group, and never to be last. Out front, you were likely to be the first to drop into the bog, and if you were last you were likely to be left behind if you fell into the bog. The place to be, I discovered, was somewhere in the middle, tucked in behind the leaders. I'm not sure how this statement stands up in assessing good leadership qualities, but the course certainly taught me the art of survival.

These management-training courses were continued over the months for all the senior managers in the company. I think the managers were more successful in building team spirit than the board had been. In fact, some of the groups still meet to go hiking, even though the people involved are now retired. To add to our enjoyment, the crafts group, as always suspicious about what everyone else was doing, became very curious and demanded to know what the secret mountain training being undertaken by management was!

One of things I discovered as my career progressed was that the further up the line you go, the less you need to know, as all around you are people who have the knowledge necessary to run each individual part of the business. The skill needed at that level is to allow the talents of other people to develop, much as the conductor does with an orchestra. In the middle-management grades, people come under great pressure from their superiors to be an authority on many aspects of the business that are not within their range of responsibility. Often, their inability to respond to their superiors on these issues can unfairly affect their future prospects in the company. When you are at the top of an organisation, it's not necessary to have all the answers, just to know where to find them. On top of that, you need a clear vision and confidence in setting the strategic targets for the organisation. While the leader can acknowledge that they do not have all the information, they must never show indecision or uncertainty, as this is guaranteed to undermine everyone's confidence.

Over the years, my predecessors, Paddy Galvin and Clive Brownlee, held annual talks with the workforce, usually in January. These talks covered the performance of the company for the previous twelve months, the group's performance internationally, and future plans and strategies. Some time before the talks, Pat Kenny came into the Brewery for a few days and spoke to as many people as he could, picking up all the gripes and complaints that people had. He would then conduct a live, taped interview with the managing director, with no cuts and no pauses, straight through. This video, of about forty-five minutes, was then played at the start of the managing director's talks and was followed by a live session of questions and answers.

These talks were extremely beneficial to me, as they gave me an opportunity to talk directly to everyone in the company, outlining future plans, threats and opportunities facing the company, and getting feedback from the grassroots. Pat Kenny's interviewing technique in the Brewery was completely different to his interviewing manner on TV. His questioning of my predecessor, Clive Brownlee, while comprehensive, had always been quite civilised, so I was taken aback when, in my first interview with him, he started by saying: 'Well, as the hatchet man of the last two [management] plans, you've now achieved your ultimate objective. What do you propose to do now?' After the interview, I confronted him about this approach, saying that I felt that he had been extremely aggressive and had treated me completely differently from my predecessor. Pat replied that the community would give him no points for adopting the same manner of questioning with me as he had with my predecessor: the interview had to match the personality! I wasn't sure whether to take that as a compliment or not!

The questions and answers at these sessions were usually quite lively. On one or two occasions, I had to restrain myself from jumping down from the stage to take a swipe at some of the more provocative audience members! On one particular occasion, having been given a particularly rough time by a group of craftsmen, I collared them at lunch and challenged them about their negative attitude. Amazingly, they were aghast at my attack and couldn't understand why I was so upset. When I indicated to them that they never had anything positive to say about the company or what we were trying to do, they retaliated by saying that it wasn't their job to be positive, it was their job to give me the problems! I told them that, being human, I sometimes needed to know that I was doing a good job or to be given reassurance, they were quite surprised and indicated that they thought I was doing a very good job but that there was no way they were going to tell me that at the talks.

I loved having the ability as managing director to use the facilities of the company for the betterment of people in the area, particularly given my background in the locality. All the members of the management team got great pleasure out of the projects we initiated and developed to help the local community.

The most successful of these projects was probably the Guinness scholarship scheme. Under this scheme, we created a number of scholarships for children in the area who might want to go on to third-level education but who would not necessarily have the funds to cover clothes, books, transport and various other incidentals. The scholarships were open to all the local schools, and the local teachers formed a committee to interview all the applicants and to put forward the successful candidates. The scheme was managed by Ada Kelly and Catherine McGoldrick on the Guinness side. They did a great job, constantly reviewing and updating the scheme.

In the first few years of the scholarship scheme, we usually had three or four scholarships; but this number was then increased to six. The scheme was later extended to cover mature people in the area who had left school and wanted to go back to study. We had a great response from the mature students and received some excellent applications for consideration.

The scholarships were presented at a dinner held in the Brewery for the successful applicants and their extended familys. Every year, we invited back the people who had been successful the year before – on their own this time – to join with the people who were being presented with scholarships on the night. It was extraordinary to notice how much those who had been in third-level education for only a year had matured. One memory that stays with me is of four former pupils of St James's CBS who, on a return visit for presentations to pupils of their school, were sitting chatting and drinking pints with the head brother, as if he was an old friend of theirs.

Another project we were involved in was one involving Sister Anthony, a nun who was working in one of the schools close to the Brewery with pre-school Traveller children. Another great initiative was the decision to open the Guinness swimming pool, at the top of Watling Street, to the local schools. Pupils in particular classes could come and be coached by our people on one morning a week to learn how to swim. Over the years, many kids in the area learnt how to swim thanks to this initiative.

During this time, we were approached by the local school-attendance officer, Michael Doyle, to see whether we would be able to help to improve the attendance in schools in the area. Together, we agreed a programme that aimed to encourage kids to attend school regularly. At the end of the year, those who had a full attendance or who had missed only a small number of days would be awarded a certificate in the Rupert Guinness Hall from the Minister for Education of the day and have their photograph taken with the Minister. This programme was a tremendous success: the rate of absenteeism from the local schools dropped dramatically. One particular family had three children getting certificates for full attendance in the first year.

Several other initiatives were undertaken, including a team of managers training young people in the area on how to start up their own business. We also had a day visit to the Brewery by a nominated class in each school. One of the best nights we had was on the occasion of a dinner for sixth-year girls to mark the closure of Basin Lane School. We had the dinner in the reception area for the class. All the girls came in looking like models, accompanied by the nuns and teachers. We had a wonderful dinner and then adjourned to the bar for lemonade. There we were, about forty of us, sitting in the bar of a brewery drinking minerals! Around midnight, we all adjourned to the brewhouse roof to see the lights of the city. As we were walking across the yard, one of the girls asked me how long I had been in the brewery. When I replied 'About thirty-eight years', she said: 'God, you must be using Oil of Ulay.' We were all invited to the girls' debs, and I went with my wife to Killiney Court Hotel to my one and only debs!

Strangely enough, although I worked in a brewery and spent a lot of my early adult life in pubs, I didn't drink by choice until I was over forty years of age. This could be a major problem when I travelled to other breweries around Europe, particularly in Germany, when visitors were generally handed huge steins of beer to sample. On one trip to Holland with a union delegation, I noticed that the level of beer in the glass of one of my colleagues, Paddy Donovan, who also didn't drink, was going down. I watched closely and discovered that, although he lifted the glass, he never drank; when he put the glass down, one of the shop stewards lifted it and drank from it!

Although I never came under pressure from anyone to drink, I felt that it wasn't fair, as personnel manager of a brewery, that I didn't sample the product. I was at dinner with the personnel director of Scottish & Newcastle Brewery in Edinburgh when I discovered that he didn't drink either. When I asked him whether he found this embarrassing, he answered by telling me that, even though his previous job was at a ladies' lingerie company, he didn't believe he should wear knickers! Nonetheless, I started to take the odd drink – although I never really acquired a taste for it. My mother, however, went to her grave still believing that her son was a teetotaller.

During this time, Guinness group head office in England decided to give employees worldwide awards for twenty-five and forty years' service. We decided to make these awards at a dinner in the Brewery for all the individuals concerned. We had so many long-service people that we ended up having three nights of dinners: many of our employees were due both the twenty-five- and forty-year awards. Each person was presented with a gift that they had chosen in advance. In addition, those receiving the twenty-five-year award were given a silver harp pin, and those receiving the forty-year award got a gold one. On those three nights, I had to smile 460 times giving out the awards! After the awards dinner, people usually adjourned to the local pubs – on many occasions leaving their canteens of cutlery or other presents behind them!

While, as managing director, running the business and ensuring the success of the company were my key tasks, the scope to make things happen and to use the company resources for good was something I missed when I left the Brewery. Nonetheless, in my capacity as chairman of Shelbourne Football Club, I was able in a smaller way to continue the practice, using the ground, the players and the structures for similar purposes.

When I initially took over as managing director, full of curiosity and interest, I walked around the plant a great deal, asking questions, looking at things and expanding my knowledge of various areas. After a few months, I realised that I was creating havoc because people were working long hours to produce figures for me on issues and items that I had queried. People were responding to my curiosity simply because I was the managing director. I didn't want people to be going to that much trouble, and certainly not in relation to casual queries on my part. As a result, I decided only to ask questions if I thought something was really important and to determine whether the information that I required was readily obtainable.

Equally, I found my freedom to move around the Brewery as managing director was more restricted than it had been when I was personnel director because, in my earlier position, it had been more acceptable for me to go from place to place. As managing director, when I wandered around people believed that there must be something wrong or that I was looking for something. All the time, they believed that there was a problem when I went visiting a section or department. Caitriona Brownlee, my predecessor's wife, told me at Clive's farewell dinner that I would find the role of MD very lonely, and completely different from being personnel director.

While most of the tasks and duties of the managing director were enjoyable, the one I really hated was the after-Christmas trip to Gleneagles, the magnificent golf hotel in Scotland, owned by Guinness. All the managing directors of the various Guinness companies around the world met there annually to be brought up to date on the group's performance. During the conference, there was a review of each country and its performance, but generally it was an exercise dominated by those around the organisation who liked to perform in front of anyone they felt could enhance their career prospects: corporate marionettes. My friend Garry McShane, the managing director of Harp, and I usually spent Christmas dreading this January expedition. The extent to which people who were so senior in the company could grovel when they were surrounded by people who were more senior to them in the organisation was remarkable. It made me wonder how the company made money; maybe it was because, as my grandmother often said, the product was made out of water!

At one of the Gleneagles conferences, the group launched 'Breakthrough', introduced by Canadian and American consultants. This was a consultancy-driven programme for the USA that was designed to improve honesty in communications in multinational environments. The programme had little impact in the already outspoken, plain-speaking environment of St James's Gate, but was exploited for personal career purposes by some in the organisation. If you were speaking the 'Breakthrough language' – such buzzwords as 'already listening', 'background conversation', 'standing in the future' were used – and were a disciple of the programme, your chances of promotion improved considerably. Indeed, it was made clear at the Gleneagles review that, while questions could be asked about Breakthrough and how it worked, it was not acceptable for people to be opposed to the programme.

I was more than a little cynical about Breakthrough. The group was adopting the programme in order to encourage people to talk to, and to be open with, each other. Imagine paying £8 million for that! Despite my antagonism, one of the consultants responsible for selling the Breakthrough concept, Josh Leibner, remains one of my best friends.


Something I had the pleasure of being involved in setting up was a roll of honour of those who had worked for Guinness and had represented their country in various sports over the years. Some of the international players had passed away, but we contacted their families and on a special night we unveiled the roll of honour in the visitors' centre. We had a tremendous turnout, including many internationals – involved in a wide variety of sports.

Never having had the opportunity of representing my country, I was envious of these people and the fact that they would be there, remembered for years to come by virtue of the fact that their names were on this big board in the visitors' centre.

There were eighty individuals representing twenty-five sports on the board. The people featured included, in soccer, Mick Leech, Martin Colfer and Liam Tuohy; in tennis, Guy Jackson and Geraldine Barnville; in swimming, Chalkie White; in boxing, Ollie Byrne, and Stephen and Terry Collins; and in athletics, Eamon Kinsella.

The next day, my secretary, Catherine McGoldrick, and Ada Kelly, who had organised the function, asked me if I was pleased to see my name on the roll of honour. They could see that I was surprised, and pointed out to me that on the bottom of the roll of honour was a little plaque indicating that I had unveiled the memorial on a particular day. As they said, my name would therefore be with the internationals for as long as the board remained. Needless to say, I was chuffed.

While the successes we achieved as a company over the years, and my involvement in turning Guinness into the most modern brewery in Europe, gave me great satisfaction, the memories of the happy occasions we celebrated with the local community and with the employees and pensioners stick in my mind more clearly. They represent a most pleasurable part of my period as managing director.

Before leaving the Brewery, I wanted to convey to the whole Guinness staff what they had achieved. With this in mind, Peter Walsh, Catherine McGoldrick and I produced a book of photographs highlighting the changes that had taken place in the Brewery over the years. The day after I left, everyone in the Brewery received a copy of the book and a letter from me thanking them for their support. The inscription inside the book reflects how I felt about our achievements. It reads:

This pictorial record of the Guinness Dublin Brewery over many, many years is a limited edition, presented to the workforce in the brewery.

It is, I hope, an enjoyable way of recording the major changes which have taken place and giving credit to the people in the brewery for having had the courage and vision to plan for the future and to implement the changes necessary to remain at the forefront of Irish and, indeed, international business. It is a record in pictorial form of how successful we have been in fighting for the investment required to bring the brewery to its current stage of leading-edge technology. The changes which have taken place and the manner of their implementation are an example to all in industry in planning at the required time and having the courage to take the necessary steps for survival and growth.

For many it will recall, with nostalgia, times long gone and will also, I think, bring home quite starkly the amount and pace of change that has taken place, particularly over the last twenty to thirty years. Most of us will recognise in the photographs various locations where we have worked or were familiar with and, indeed, people we knew over a long period.

There are many photographs from which we could have selected but we hope that the ones we have selected aptly record in visual terms the extent of what has been achieved. It is a history of change, courage and vision but most of all, pride.

*October 1994*

\*

In the fifties and sixties, Guinness was a traditional, somewhat arrogant and dominant company. It operated in a very protected environment and made good profits without ever having to be at the leading edge of new technology or even of best management practice. The company had for many years been producing a product that basically sold itself: there was very little competition, particularly in Ireland, and drinkers who started drinking Guinness in their twenties often remained loyal to the product for life. In short, the company had become old-fashioned and uncommercial, with rising unit costs, falling sales and dwindling profits.

In addition to being brewed in Ireland, Guinness was also produced in sixteen breweries, located in seven countries, around the world, with the concentrate provided from Dublin. It was also brewed under contract in forty-five other countries and sold in a hundred and forty markets around the world. The Irish economy gained to the tune of £350 million in excise duty and VAT every year and a further £200 million was spent on purchases of barley and other goods in Ireland. The feeling in Guinness was that the company would not face the problems and turmoil that other companies encountered. By and large, life in the Brewery was extremely relaxed, cosy and comfortable.

At the time, nearly four thousand people were employed full-time in the Brewery at St James's Gate, and between three hundred and five hundred people were employed on a casual basis. The perception was that anyone who came to do a once-off job in the Brewery – such as painting, plumbing or repairing – was kept on forever.

As many of the senior managers saw their post in Guinness as a reward for their previous service to the British Empire, there was little in the way of real business-management experience in the organisation. This mattered little as long as the company experienced few problems. The 1974 strike brought home to the board the fragmentation that existed across the company and the impact of this fragmentation on the way in which the business was run. The lack of communication across the various groups made dealing with the most basic issues extremely difficult. The company, with its paternalistic attitude, its rigid divisions, and a product that sold itself, had never before had to face up to a trauma of this kind. The company was clearly entering uncharted waters.

Following the strike, a tribunal, set up under the auspices of the Labour Court, proposed the formation of a Brewery Council to break down the barriers that existed across the company. The strength of the union and its growth in the company was a new feature of the company which the board would have to take more seriously. The board would also have to develop a more inclusive workforce and to promote managers who had the ability to deal directly with the union. This change was probably another stroke of luck for me, as it pushed me into the forefront of the industrial-relations field.

During this period another major business problem appeared on the horizon, with the emergence of light beers and the development of the lager market. It was clear that 'black beer' was under threat. Indeed, in the early eighties production of Guinness in Dublin dropped by about 10 percent due not only to the swing towards so-called bright beers but also to inflation, which meant that people had less money to spend. In addition, the proliferation of products in the alcoholic-drinks market was making the consumer less loyal and more likely to experiment.

The early seventies saw the start of a change for the Brewery in Dublin following a proposal to build a brewery in the north of England to supply the British trade, because of the widening gap in productivity between Dublin and other breweries in Britain and elsewhere around the world. Guinness Dublin at that stage depended on the British trade for 40 percent of its production. As a result of the threat that this proposal represented, the Development Plan was hastily put together by the Irish management led by Guy Jackson, who was one of those killed in the Staines Air Crash in 1972. This plan outlined a range of proposals to reduce costs, including compulsory retirement and reductions in numbers by about 1,500 employees, with compulsory early retirement at fifty-five for shop-floor workers.

Given the climate that had prevailed up to then in the company – people were guaranteed employment to sixty-five, and there was a womb-to-tomb mentality – the Development Plan came as a major shock to many within the organisation. Some people were simply unable to cope with the situation. In fact, I met several employees outside the Brewery who cried and said that they would have worked for nothing in the company because they missed the camaraderie, the craic, and the other day-to-day benefits of going to work.

It is difficult to envisage today that people would be reluctant to go on early retirement, given that early retirement has become common and even desirable. Over the years, Guinness people went from the trauma of the Development Plan and a feeling that they were being thrown onto the scrapheap if they took early retirement, to accepting that their working life and their life as a retired person were separate things.

At the time of the Development Plan, no preparation had been made to help people adjust to retirement, and the sudden impact of retirement on the secure lives of Guinness employees left many traumatised. Nonetheless, the plan put forward to the main Guinness board in England retained the British trade, under guarantee, for twenty years.

The Development Plan also involved a £30 million investment in new plant between 1971 and 1976 and resulted in the workforce being reduced from 4,000 permanent jobs and 1,500 daily casual employees to 2,500 in total over a five-year period. The programme included compulsory retirement at fifty-five for non-management people. For two centuries, the company had been known for its paternalistic care for its employees and the high standards of wages and fringe benefits, and the high degree of job security, it offered.

Implementation of the plan also meant that those who stayed had to take on the work of those who had left, usually by working overtime. As a result, overtime became institutionalised: it became an accepted part of the individual's pay packet.

By the early eighties, however, it was clear that the lack of investment in the St James's Gate brewery over the years was seriously threatening its future. Over €140 million was required to rebuild the Brewery, and a new plan, the Future Competitiveness Plan (FCP), was devised. This plan saw savings across all operations and further reductions of 1,000 people, to 1,500, as well as many changes in work practices.

The plan required the old brewery to continue to brew while at the same time new plant and new technology were introduced on site. The plan brought severe strain into the system, because for a long period we were operating two breweries, the old and the new, while simultaneously reducing the workforce. Although this in itself was a major achievement, when the new plant was up and running, we ran into significant technical difficulties. Some managers, fearing that we might not be able to brew to the quality Guinness required, began to despair. This fear quickly passed, however, as the technical team got to grips with the problems and the plant went on to produce excellent-quality Guinness.

St James's Gate gradually became one of the most modern breweries in the world. The management of other breweries in Japan, Germany, America and elsewhere came to Dublin to observe and learn from what we had achieved. We had a creative and innovative group of managers, in both brewing and engineering, who designed and maintained the modern plant and equipment we required. Given the way in which the Guinness Group has evolved since then, it is unlikely that Dublin would today receive the type of investment that was made in it at that time. Whereas in the eighties nearly 70 percent of the group's profits came from Ireland, the distilling side of the business is now the major contributor of profits.

Although the FCP was a success, one of the lessons we learned from its implementation was that the world does not stand still. While FCP ensured the survival of the Brewery, our competitors, both inside and outside the Guinness Group, had continued to improve their efficiency levels and work practices. As a result, in 1987, at which time we had only just finished implementing FCP, circumstances changed again.

From being a large, single-product, single-site company, we had become part of a diversified multinational corporation, with a strong marketing presence in all parts of the globe. The takeover by Guinness of United Distillers and a number of smaller distilling and brewing companies had resulted in a situation where brewing made up only about 20 percent of the total profits of the groups. From being the major company of the group, we were suddenly just one unit amongst many, all competing for new products and new investment. The structure of the group had changed so dramatically that the Irish operation, which had previously made up to 70 percent of the group profits now contributed 8 percent, even though it was making more money than ever before.

By the late eighties, the company was a multinational. After the then managing director, Ernest Saunders, took over Distillers and Bells, we were now part of a global organisation. We realised that there was a requirement for us to examine further our costs and to cut out all non-essential services.

Our strong point had always been that we planned from a position of strength and were often ahead of the posse in this regard. We were, at that time, ahead of most companies in deciding to discontinue all non-core business and instead to contract them out. We had our own security, catering and ships, and these were quite a burden on the unit costs of producing in Dublin. In addition, we still had a large engineering department. At one stage, this department employed in excess of nine hundred people – more than ran the whole brewery when I left in 1994. Some people said that we were an engineering company that produced beer!

In addition, we had to take into consideration the fact that, uniquely, we provided a free medical department, with dentists, doctors, physiotherapists, pharmacists, nurses and a social worker, and that all meals were provided for members of staff free of charge. As a result, our costs were out of line with competitor breweries both inside and outside the Guinness Group.

Yet another plan, the Continuing Competitiveness Plan (CCP), was drawn up. As part of this plan, we decided to contract out security and catering, as well as the management of the Guinness ships. This plan was in many ways the most difficult to sell to the workforce because it was not based on the need for survival, as had been the case with the Development Plan, or on the need to fund a £100 million–plus investment programme, as had been the case with the FCP. Instead, the CCP was based on the need for Guinness Dublin to become more commercially viable within a large group. The trouble with any plan based on contracting out non-core activities is that the jobs are still there to be done by somebody else, while people are being asked to leave by way of redundancy programmes. Agreement to the plan was reached, however, and the CCP was implemented.

The Personnel Division achieved most of its proposed savings within the first few months of the Plan. Seventy percent of our proposals had been agreed, despite the fact that we had the biggest numbers to achieve and the most difficult negotiations, in that we were contracting out security and catering, two major divisions of the company.

In addition to managing a line department of seven hundred people, as personnel director I was also responsible for the personnel policies necessary to facilitate the major change programmes. It wasn't just the implementation of the various plans that made Personnel an exciting place to work: during my time as personnel manager, we had a great team of people and had some fabulous laughs. Coffee time with Victor Leeson, now unfortunately deceased, of the Guinness Choir, and Paddy Maher were something else. Paddy and Victor were charged with managing our massive redeployment programme, moving hundreds of employees to jobs around the Brewery. They often claimed that they were involved in moving phantom armies around the site. This exercise has, I hope, prepared me for my current role as chairman of the Government's Decentralisation Implementation Group!

We were entertained by Paddy and Victor most mornings, sometimes for only five minutes if there was a crisis, or for an hour if things were more relaxed. While we were not aware of it at the time, these moments probably did more to consolidate team spirit and build relationships than any formal training could have done.

Managers seem to relax very little these days. Every minute must be focused on business, every meeting has a purpose, and every time a manager talks to someone he or she is looking for something. As a result, they often don't have time to get to know their staff and are always racing against deadlines.

Sometimes the confrontation across the negotiating table was not the only problem. In 1988, the Guinness switchboard took a phone call from someone who made a death threat against me. Unfortunately, the newspapers got wind of this and printed the story without naming 'the executive' involved. My poor mother read about the case in the papers and was most concerned for the poor man's family – never even thinking that the preson involved might be me! For some time, this threat dominated my life: I had to be careful everywhere I went and to listen carefully to Garda advice.

This was a period of great achievement for the Personnel Department, both as a line department with responsibility for hundreds of employees and also in terms of the formulation of policy. We in the department felt that we were achieving a great deal: although we worked all the hours God sent and were frustrated on many occasions, there was a real buzz about the place.

During the implementation of most of these plans, the management team tended to congregate in one specific office in the building, dubbed 'NASA Control', particularly when the plans went wrong or if anything serious was taking place. One such important occasion was when the registration of our ships had been transferred from Britain to Ireland in order to hand over the management to a company formed by former employees of Irish Shipping; the first ship was to sail under the Irish flag rather than, as heretofore, under the Union Jack. We all sat in the office in anticipation of hearing that everything had gone well and that the ship had sailed, fully laden.

On hearing nothing for an hour after the estimated time of departure, and having failed to make contact with the ship by phone, we sent scouts down to the quays to see what was happening. When they got there, they found that there was a picket on the fully laden ship. We were in the worst possible situation: having transferred the registration of the ships from Britain to

Ireland, we couldn't transfer it back. Moreover, our crew was gone, and we couldn't supply the British trade. Needless to say, the strike placed great strains on the systems we had in place, and it did nothing for our image across the water. The dispute was resolved after three months by the intervention of the Irish Congress of Trades Union, which brokered a settlement.

The Continuing Competitiveness Plan reduced the workforce to less than nine hundred and led to the contracting out of all the non-core activities: catering, security, shipping and some elements of craft work. We were left to concentrate on running the Brewery and producing high-quality Guinness at the right price, at the right time, for our customers both at home in Ireland and around the world.

At this stage, the St James's Gate Brewery had been involved in constant and dramatic changes for a period of twenty years. We had seen many changes: from the old barges moving up and down the Liffey to 'silver bullets' – the road tankers that carried the product up and down the quays – from cargo ships to tanker ships, from wooden casks to steel kegs, from a very labour-intensive operation to a highly automated plant, all in a relatively short space of time. We had turned the company from a slumbering giant which had become old-fashioned and uncommercial into a modern industrial giant which had world-class technology, quality assurance and cost control and was seen as being in the forefront of European business.

All of these changes had brought a great deal of pain and anguish to many people, however. Apart from the number of jobs at Guinness having been reduced dramatically – from four thousand to a mere nine hundred – the old family tradition of a father being followed into the Brewery by his son or daughter had been broken. Guinness now had more pensioners than employees, and as a result people had to work harder than in the past. We had to change our management style and management structures on many occasions in order to remain competitive. Nonetheless, we had secured the future for the Dublin brewery, at least for the time being and had also managed to hold on to our export trade. In short, we were now part of a very success-ful multinational company. Worldwide, however, the pace of change continued. As a result, we entered into Plan 2000, a rev-olutionary plan to ensure the continued survival of the St James's Gate Brewery.

By now, St James's Gate had developed a good reputation for managing change and was seen as being very competitive when benchmarked against other operations around the world, both within and outside the group. In early 1992, I went to the Irish Management Institute to give a talk on managing change and leadership. I included – as I always did in such talks – a reference to chief executives who left their organisations in what appeared to be a healthy state, while they themselves were aware that the company was heading for trouble. Invariably, not long after such a chief executive left the company, major problems surfaced for the organisation, mainly because the departing chief executive had at some stage taken a soft option rather than making diffi-cult strategic decisions before leaving. In many cases, these indi-viduals left the impression that they had achieved a lot, whereas in fact, in some cases, as a result of their inaction they had ensured the company's demise.

At this stage, I was fairly clear that the Guinness organisation in which I had grown up was changing in a way that I didn't like. I came to the view that I no longer wanted to be a part of the company in the long term and began to think about moving on. In fact, I began to put into practice the theory I had been expounding in the IMI: that people at the top of organisations had a responsibility to ensure the future of their organisations, even after they had gone.

The reason for my concerns was that I believed, at the time, that Guinness did not need to be in Ireland into the next centu-ry. I believed that Guinness might pull out of Ireland altogether and brew primarily in the UK for the British and Irish markets. I came to this conclusion based on the fact that, while we were making around £150 million profit in Ireland at the time, £70 million of this figure was being made from the concentrate sold to breweries around the world that were producing Guinness, and a significant amount was being earned by the sales of Guinness into the British trade. Both of these markets could be supplied from anywhere – it didn't have to be from Ireland.

Some of my management colleagues argued that, if Guinness left Ireland, there would be a boycott of the products in Ireland and that the company would lose around £50 million as a result. At that stage, however, we were looking at an organisation that was heading for huge profits, and therefore the loss of £50 million, while substantial, would not be a disaster, particularly if significant savings could be made.

Put bluntly, if the group was to rationalise production into one location, possibly outside Ireland, it could make huge savings. The sixty-acre James's Gate site in Dublin would be a prime development target, worth many millions. It was accepted by the Dublin board that this was a real possibility, and we were conscious of the disastrous effect that Guinness leaving Ireland would have on the Irish economy. With this in mind, the management team agreed to produce a plan that would make it extremely difficult for the group to move production out of Ireland.

Initially, we delegated two senior managers to examine what was happening in other businesses, and particularly in other breweries, and to report back to the senior management group in the company. Out of this project came the proposals for Plan 2000, which was basically a plan to increase the production of the Guinness Dublin Brewery from four million hectolitres per year to six million hectolitres, at the lowest feasible capital cost.

In putting together this plan, we had an edge over other operations in the group because our technical people, in brewing, engineering and finance, were extremely creative. They came up with proposals that would enable us to brew an extra 2 million hectolitres for a capital investment of only £30 million.

When the plan was put to people in head office in Britain, the then head of Guinness brewing worldwide, Brian Baldock, insisted at a meeting that there was no way he would put all his eggs in one basket and that brewing Guinness solely out of

Dublin was a non-starter. At the time, I remember thinking that, while it was his prerogative to make that decision, over the years he would have more and more difficulty explaining to the shareholders why an opportunity to close Park Royal Brewery in London and sell the land for something between £150 million and £200 million was being ignored, particularly as the brewing capacity of Park Royal could, as we were showing, be replaced for a mere £30 million in Dublin.

Nonetheless, mindful that our chances of achieving our goal depended on instilling confidence in the decision-makers at group level, we set about negotiating a new type of plan. We were conscious that we could not afford to put the group in a 'ransom situation' – as we would be doing if all the Guinness was being brewed in Dublin.

Plan 2000 was based on a contract between employees and management to move away from the normal processes of negotiating change to a situation where management could instantly, speedily and flexibly respond to the requirements of the Guinness Group. This freedom for management would require safeguards to be given to the employees regarding their future. While we in Ireland saw ourselves as being successful in achieving agreement to change and had a reputation for creating a consensus, it was clear that, in the changing business world, this would not be enough. Negotiations were frequently protracted: by the time agreement had been achieved, it was too late, and too much money had been spent. For multinational companies in particular, this was – and will continue to be – a major problem. It is often the case that head office doesn't care about local problems or practices, it just wants action – yesterday.

Part of our management strategy to have the extra production done in Dublin included all the senior management people, when they went to visit the outposts of the Guinness 'empire' in Nigeria, Cameroon, Ghana and Britain, constantly referring to the fact that Guinness Dublin could increase its output by 50 percent for an investment of just £30 million. The aim of this 'hijacking' of the PR system within the group was to ensure that decision-makers within the group heard about our plan and began to ask questions why it was not being looked at seriously.

The requirement to manage PR within an organisation is extremely important in an international company, where people sitting in an office in Europe or America make decisions that can result in the wiping out of an operation elsewhere with the stroke of a pen.

While I was chairman of the Labour Court, having left Guinness in 1994, I was sent a note about a board meeting in London where it was noted that Guinness Dublin should make itself available to move up to production of 6 million hectolitres. What Guinness Dublin had set out to achieve in 1992, it was now being instructed to implement! This gave me great satisfaction. Moreover, in 2004 it was announced that Park Royal would close and that Guinness Dublin would take over its brewing.

This is the direct consequence of Plan 2000, which, although devised in the early nineties, has only now come to fruition. The implementation of this plan is an example of people planning for the future, even though they would not be around to see the fulfilment of their plans. In this case, most of the managers who were involved in creating Plan 2000 in 1992 had left the company in the meantime. In true corporate fashion, however, nobody will remember how the original idea for Plan 2000 was conceived or how everything was put together to make it happen!


The Ernest Saunders era at Guinness was a traumatic experience for those who were affected by his actions. The period between 1981, when he took over, to his resignation in 1987 was a roller coaster for everyone involved. It seemed to me that Saunders did not pay as much attention to the Guinness operation in Ireland as he did to the British operation. Nevertheless, the Irish operation was affected by the presence of his consultants from the Baines Group, known as 'the Bainies'. These consultants took up residence in Ireland for a period of time, putting pressure on the management to reduce costs even further than according to the terms of the plans that were already in position. There were regular confrontations between some operating managers and the consultants, in relation to decisions on running the business. Indeed, I remember on one occasion Paddy Galvin threatening one of the Bainies with physical violence if he opened his mouth at one meeting.

Personally, I suffered no ill effects from the Saunders era, except that when I was personnel director Saunders decided that the bonus of four weeks' pay given to everybody at Christmas, would no longer be paid in cash but in shares. The task of selling this to the workforce, where most employees' plans for the Christmas season centred on receipt of this money and where a lot of the major shops in Dublin planned their sales around the 'Guinness payment', was not to be taken lightly. Having spent many weeks persuading employees that this was a positive step, as the company would continue to grow in the future, the unions reluctantly agreed to accept the change. Their acceptance of it was mainly based on a deal we did with them to give them cash – equivalent to the net money they would have received – in the form a loan, to be paid back when the shares could be exercised, without adverse tax implications, five years hence. We agreed to do this for five consecutive years; in the sixth year, the money had to be paid back whether people decided to sell their shares or not. All of this was done without the knowledge of head office in the UK: they would have felt the change in arrangements for payment of the Christmas bonus was an item not for negotiation but for implementation.

Things ran smoothly until Saunders was charged in relation to inappropriate share dealing with regard to the takeover of Distillers and Bell. When this cash proposal, relating to the Christmas bonus, was being sold to the union, the Guinness share price had been £3.26. However, shortly after the introduction of the new scheme, because of the Saunders situation, the share price plummeted to £2.76. I had many unhappy people knocking at my door asking where the positive aspect of this deal was. Subsequently, the same share price went as high as £12 over a very short period, and everyone gained significantly. Most of our employees referred to the stock-exchange reports on a daily basis during these exciting years.

Saunders had never really got to grips with the Irish situation directly; on the other hand, almost every senior manager in the British operation had been replaced during his tenure. On one of the occasions that Saunders came to Ireland – to mark the opening of a new plant in the Harp brewery in Dundalk – the Guinness security people in Britain, believing that Dundalk was in the north of Ireland, wanted to ensure that the RUC were there to protect them! Such were the changes that had taken place in our organisation!

The transformation of Guinness, with the acquisition of Distillers and Bells, into the Diageo company, has been quite a traumatic one for many Guinness people, as the takeover of Distillers by Guinness had been for the Distillers people. I met many of the Distillers staff at various conferences after the Guinness takeover, and they were extremely angry with and critical of their senior management because they had allowed the smaller Guinness company to take them over. The subsequent creation of the new company, Diageo, was seen by many in the Guinness organisation as being the final straw. These people saw this change as marking a diminishing of the status of Guinness and believed that it would result in a change of culture at the company. Guinness went from being the big company within the group, to being a smaller fish in a bigger pond. Over a period of time, the majority of the people in Guinness in Ireland with long service retired from the company; those who have come into the company since see themselves – quite correctly – as Diageo employees.

In my own case, I had become aware of the change coming in the organisation I had grown up with, and which I loved. I saw that the values that were likely to apply in the new company would be alien to everything I believed in. The company was now operating as a multinational, and the perceptions of those at the headquarters in England were that the 'outposts' – particularly the Irish side of the business – were not to be trusted.

The amalgamation of companies and cultures today as a result of the globalisation of business means that conflicts similar to those experienced within Guinness and Distillers in the creation of Diageo will arise as companies reorganise and restructure. People who have particularly long service with companies see this long service turning from a positive factor to a negative one – something that is difficult for them to understand. The change from long-term service to short-term contracts is a major problem in building trust. The fact that people on three- to five-year contracts make key decisions on behalf of the company – decisions the results of which they will not be around to witness directly – does not inspire confidence in employees who have been with the company for the long haul. In general, however, younger workers are attracted by short-term contacts, and indeed often enjoy moving between companies. They have the confidence that they can pick up comparable – or better – posts as they move across the business world. They often seem not to believe, as longer-serving employees did, that companies have a 'heart', and as a result these people may be less affected at an emotional level by the actions of a particular company.

The Guinness organisation in Ireland over the years has been an excellent example of managing change. In all of the major change programmes that were implemented – moving the organisation through a compulsory-retirement programme, implementing voluntary-retirement programmes, rebuilding the entire organisation, managing significant capital projects and changing the culture of the organisation – there was no disruption to trade and no strikes as a result of the programmes. The other satisfying feature of the change programmes was that they were implemented in what I would describe as 'the Guinness way'. Apart from the Development Plan, they were handled in a humane way: people were treated well and continued to feel, even after they had left, that they were part of the company. This situation manifests itself in a number of ways, including in the fact that the Guinness pensioners are still entitled to go into the Brewery every day for a free lunch, and to use the facilities of the Medical Department. Unfortunately, many Guinness people still hanker after the Guinness company that they knew. These people have not yet accepted that Guinness is now a product rather than a company, and that the company as they knew it is gone.

Personally, having decided to leave Guinness, I made my intentions known in the wider business world. Subsequently, before my resignation, I was offered the post of deputy chairman of the Labour Court, leading to my appointment as chairman in 1994. So it was that, at the age of fifty-five, having completed forty-one years of service at St James's Gate, I headed for Haddington Road and the Labour Court, thereby moving from the private to the public sector and becoming the first chairman of the court from the private sector.

3

## The Labour Court

Arriving in the Labour Court in 1994 was a new start for me, after the politics of a big organisation such as Guinness. The pressure of operating in a multinational, where the perceptions of those at the centre were that the outposts, particularly the Irish side of the business, were not to be trusted, made things quite stressful. The court, with its friendly atmosphere, lack of politics and focus purely on the business in hand – the resolution of disputes – was a breath of fresh air.

Before I retired from Guinness in 1994, I spoke to John Dunne, director general of IBEC, and told him of my intention to leave Guinness. He asked at the time if I would consider going into the Labour Court as deputy chairman if I was offered the position. The idea didn't appeal to me at all. While I said that I would think about it, I really didn't see this as a route I wanted to travel. However, after further discussion with my wife Anne and with John, I indicated my interest in the post, subject to having a commitment that I would later become chairman. I was subsequently appointed deputy chairman and told that, when Evelyn Owens, the incoming chairman, retired in four years' time, I would become chairman.

Coming from a situation where I was running a company that was a seven-day-a-week, twenty-four-hour-a-day operation, to a situation where I went home at a reasonable time – apart from the occasions when disputes necessitated working late into the night – was extremely refreshing. Having been at the centre of all this activity for years, it was also a major challenge for me not to get directly involved in the cases being heard by the court. To sit and listen, statesmanlike, to the submissions made by both sides, without intervening on occasions to shout 'That's a lie!' took a supreme effort on my part.

Every morning for months, when I went out to work my wife reminded me that there were people coming to the court that day who had possibly been awake all night worrying about the fact that they had to attend. That is something that can easily be overlooked – the tensions and stresses on people, no matter how informal the court tries to be. Having been before the court in my previous job as personnel director in Guinness, and having had to sit there and put up with the questioning of the 'three wise people' on the bench, I was only too conscious of the difficulties that were involved for people who were coming in to present their cases.

A welcome new experience was the variety of cases with which I was dealing. I was now involved in a wide range of cases dealing with all sorts of industrial disputes, equality issues and sexual-harassment cases, while familiarising myself with the wide range of business sectors in the country. One of the benefits of working in the court was that, in the submissions made by the parties to a dispute, we got not only the outline of the dispute but also a comprehensive briefing of the business sector in which the company operated. Many cases gave us a worldwide appreciation of various business sectors.

From the beginning, I was very impressed with the professionalism of those appearing in the court and the standard of their submissions. With one or two exceptions, most of the submissions were clear and to the point, and relatively complicated cases were argued extremely ably. The occasional lengthy submission, while frequently the personal trait of a particular individual, more often indicated that there was very little substance to the arguments being made and that the submission was padded out with all sorts of irrelevant and unnecessary information. Equally, the verbal presentations of most of those attending the court were extremely articulate and professional and dealt with the issues concisely – although a few did wander all over the place. Sometimes, the union side went back to 1913, while management, when arguing their inability to pay, often only just stopped short of taking up a collection!

Frequently, one side would send its submission into the court before the other. When reading the submission, I would often think: this is an open-and-shut case, the other side has no chance. When the second submission was read, however, a completely different impression was gained. I became used to waiting in anticipation for the second version of events!

Since the establishment of the Labour Relations Commission in 1990, there has been confusion between what it does and what the role of the Labour Court is. There is even confusion in the minds of some of the industrial-relations correspondents as to how the structures of the State's industrial-relations machinery operate. The Labour Relations Commission's role in disputes is basically to try to get the parties to conciliate and, where possible, to reach agreement. If they fail to do so, the issue is then passed on, by agreement of the parties, to the Labour Court, which will then hear the case based on written and oral submissions and will make a recommendation for settlement.

The chairman and the two deputy chairmen are appointed by the Minister for Enterprise, Trade and Employment. The Minister also appoints the Labour Court's legal adviser – the registrar. The employers' members are nominated by IBEC (the Irish Business and Employers' Confederation), and the workers' members are nominated by ICTU (the Irish Congress of Trade Unions).

The public and indeed the parties to particular high-profile cases seem to believe that a division has only that one case to deal with when formulating a recommendation. The reality, however, is that the 'division' of the court (a division consists of one employer member, one worker member and the independent chair) may be dealing with anything up to a dozen cases at any one time.

Before making its recommendation, a division will consider the oral and written evidence presented and try to arrive at a consensus. If consensus cannot be reached, the chairman will make the decision. All three members of the court are bound by the decision of the division on the day, however, and no one can disassociate themselves from the recommendation. This last element is a very important part of the court's operation and has stood to the court over many years, in some extremely difficult cases. It has been honoured by all the members and has enabled the court to gain the reputation it enjoys for fairness, integrity and professionalism.

Once a division makes its decision after hearing a case, it is the role of the chairman to write up the recommendation. This, again, was a whole new experience for me, as I had come from an organisation where other people were available to me to write up reports or supply whatever information I needed. I now found myself having to produce my own reports, in the form of recommendations. It was also a new experience for me to produce recommendations that, when accepted, would have to be implemented by some other poor soul.

One aspect of my role that I found difficult to accept initially was having to get consensus from my division. Having always had problems when I was not the one making the decisions, it was particularly trying for me to have to work at reaching a consensus on various decisions among my tribunal colleagues.

With the proliferation of labour legislation and regulations, and the increase in European legislation in the workplace, many of the issues coming to the court are now of a legalistic nature. These cases can be extremely complex and take up an increasing amount of the court's time. One equality case could take the same amount of the court's time as half a dozen industrial-relations cases. Equality determinations have to be written bearing in mind that they may be appealed on to the legal courts. They need to be written in such a way as to ensure that, on appeal, the decision of the Labour Court is upheld.

In any one year, the court handles up to eight hundred cases, but only a few of these cases are reported in the media. While, over the years, the tradition has been that the chairman takes the high-profile cases, sometimes a case can become high profile without warning. One such case arose for me shortly after I joined the court: the Dunnes Stores dispute. This dispute, which centred on the so-called zero-option contract and Sunday working, had major ramifications throughout the retail trade. People could be rostered to work at any time in the week but were not guaranteed any hours of work. If an employee did not come in when called, it was claimed that they were unlikely to be called again. The union was looking for a specified minimum number of hours and other concessions.

It was during this case that I learned that the timing of interventions and the issuing of recommendations were very important when trying to resolve disputes. In the Dunnes case, it was clear that the good weather being enjoyed across the country in July 1995 was distracting people from the task of seeking a resolution of the dispute. As I travelled around the country to various Labour Court sittings in Cork, Galway, Tralee and Limerick, I passed Dunnes Stores staff sitting in the sun getting a tan. Although people were obviously worried about being on strike, the weather was a great tranquilliser!

We had been working on a possible solution, and we produced a recommendation just as the weather broke. Although I'm not saying that the weather breaking resolved the Dunnes dispute, it certainly helped to get people to look more seriously at the proposals. In this case, the weather changing probably gave us a couple of hundred more votes for acceptance of the proposals.

The resolution of the strike ended one of the most emotive disputes that had been seen in Ireland in years. It saw very high levels of public support for those on the picket line, and prominent members of the Catholic hierarchy taking the workers' side. It was estimated, but never confirmed, that Dunnes had lost about £1 million in turnover a day, while Mandate was reputed to have paid out £750,000 in strike pay to their members who were on the picket line.

The ending of the strike brought about change in Dunnes Stores' handling of its business: after initial criticisms in the press, it employed a PR company and also abandoned its long-standing policy of not attending the Labour Court.

Initially, as deputy chairman I had to learn to adjust to a different pace and way of life. I found the approach of the court, a combination of the formal and the informal, confusing at times. We were projecting an image of informality while, at the same time, when the court members entered the room, everybody stood up. The representatives of the parties also stood when making their submissions to the court. I found all this difficult to take in the beginning, but over time I came to realise that the formality of some aspects of the court's operations was necessary to avoid anarchy and to maintain the dignity of the court. Having had to order someone who had approached the bench in a threatening manner to return to his seat, I became convinced as to the appropriateness of the procedures!

The power of the bench is paramount, and the chairman of the division must control the proceedings to ensure that the parties have every opportunity to present their cases. This is particularly relevant where one party tries to verbally assault the other side across the courtroom. Sometimes, when legal people are in attendance, they are inclined to adopt this more legal, adversarial approach, which is not acceptable in the Labour Court.

From the outset, I was impressed with the courage of individuals who, without representation, came into the court and presented their own case, often facing a battery of barristers, solicitors and directors of companies. Frequently, individuals won their case without having incurred any of the costs that would apply to the other side. If people present their case factually and accurately, and have merit in their case, their chances of winning are as good as people who spend significant amounts of money on representation. That is one of the great benefits of the Labour Court.

When I took over as chairman of the Labour Court in 1998, I was surprised when Kevin Duffy informed me that I was the first-ever chairman to come from the private sector. To be appointed chairman of the Labour Court was a tremendous honour and a great challenge, given the national profile the Court had gained over fifty years, and its standing in the eyes of the public.

On the Marian Finucane radio programme after my appointment, Marian introduced me as the man with one of the worst jobs in Ireland. I think she was taken aback when I disagreed with her and said that I had a brilliant job, which I loved! The job was even more attractive to me as I had no direct boss, I told her. While the Department of Enterprise, Trade and Employment has responsibility for the administration and day-to-day operations of the Labour Court, the court has complete freedom in relation to its handling of disputes, within the legislative guidelines.

The paranoia of practitioners, politicians and others not to be seen to interfere with the court leaves the court in a unique position of independence. While this independence is necessary to ensure that the court can operate, with it of course comes responsibility – particularly taking into account that the court's recommendations can have a major effect not only on companies and workers but also on the economy.

When I became chairman of the court, full of enthusiasm, just as I had been initially as managing director in my days in Guinness, I decided to do a complete review of every activity and operation in the court. Fifteen project teams were set up to examine the various sectors, particularly those that affected the smooth running of the court, its financial and administrative performance, and the service it provided to its clients.

This was a new experience for the members of the court and for the staff, but everyone entered into it with enthusiasm, and the findings of the teams resulted in a number of very useful proposals to improve the operation of the court. One of the main proposals coming out of the exercise was to have all recommendations, other than the equality cases, issued within twenty-one days. This was implemented, and we achieved a success rate of 80 percent. Another improvement we made was in the linkages between the court, the Construction Industry Federation, the Construction Monitoring Board, and the Labour Inspectorate to speed up the inspections of companies that had been reported for being in breach of the pension requirements.

A major source of annoyance over many years had been the constant problems faced by our programming section when trying to get parties to agree dates for hearings. If a company was looking for something from the employees, the union usually made itself scarce. On the other hand, if the union was making a claim on the company, the company became unavailable. This resulted in programming staff spending a huge amount of time trying to get the parties to agree a date for a hearing.

Arising out of the project review, we introduced a 'two strikes and out' policy to put an end to this merry-go-round. This policy meant that, if either party turned down two dates, a date was imposed, and the hearing went ahead on that date with no option for a postponement. This policy was extremely successful and considerably improved the delay time in cases going through the court. However, one union official refused to come in on an imposed date, claiming that what we were doing was unconstitutional!

At this time, the court did not have its own budget; it was provided with the necessary resources and finances by the Department of Enterprise, Trade and Employment. In discussions with the finance section of the Department, it was agreed that the Labour Court would have its own budget and be responsible for managing its own expenditure.

Very early in this process, I learned the pitfalls of managing my own budget in the public sector: the practice appeared to be that, every year, the government looked for a percentage cut on the previous year's spend rather than on the previous year's budget. This meant that, if you had been efficient and prudent and come in under budget, you were screwed even more the following year. The effect of this kind of budgetary control, as I had seen in Guinness, was that people made sure to spend up to their budget limit and therefore had an easier ride in the next year.

After discussions between the finance section and ourselves, it was agreed that a more realistic approach would be taken to budgeting and that we would be allowed to use the savings we had made, in other areas. This, we were told, was a major break-through!

As chairman of the court, I adopted the same approach as I had in Guinness, in projecting the court nationally at various seminars and conferences. Early in my tenure, I presented a paper to a conference in UCD which basically looked for a com-plete review of all of the State's industrial-relations machinery, with a view to ensuring that it was appropriate for the next ten years. I suggested that this review should also take into account the non-users of the court, who appeared to be very successful in running their business, in order to see if the institutions could learn from them.

This paper was not well received, particularly by IBEC, with the result that no review took place. In the months before I retired from the court, however, a government review did take place, and recommendations have now been made in relation to the operations of the Employment Appeals Tribunal, the Equality Agency, the Labour Relations Commission and the Labour Court.

The reputation and high standing of the court has been greatly enhanced by the fact that members of the court are respected as experienced practitioners in their own right and because, over the years, the court has consistently succeeded in resolving the most difficult industrial-relations disputes. Despite the voluntary nature of acceptance of the court's recommenda-tions, the acceptance rate is more than 80 percent.

When we met our counterparts in the USA, they told us that their acceptance rate on recommendations was only 47 percent. My belief is that our high rate of acceptance is down to the fact that members of the court have been practitioners and have come into the court with good track records of achievement, built up over many years. In the USA, by contrast, the Labour Court is made up entirely of legal experts.

The make-up of the members of the court is a very important factor in its smooth operation, and it is therefore essential that people of the right calibre are selected to be members. The role requires experience, drive, patience and the ability to listen. Members must make sure they are au fait with what is happening in the world of business, and in industry generally. They must be prepared to study the legislation and to keep up to date with any changes. Perhaps there should be a requirement for them to go back into industry for periods of six months during their tenure, but this may not be practical. Members should, in my view, be in the court for a maximum of seven years, as they can become remote from the business world over a lengthy period of time.

The government's decision to break with the tradition of appointing as chairman the deputy chairman of the court, when Kevin Duffy became chairman on my retirement, may signal a change in thinking in relation to the selection of court members. It is opportune to review not just the time that members spend in the court but also the training and updating of their knowledge.

Labour Court recommendations had over the years been signed by one person – in recent times, by the chairman. Some members of the court felt that, because of this, the media tended to report cases as if only the chairman had heard the case. In order to rectify this, it was agreed that the names of the members of the relevant division would appear on the recommendations. Unfortunately, while this solved one problem, it made the members more personally vulnerable to criticism when people disagreed with a particular recommendation.

While the court's primary objective is to produce settlements in disputes, I have always had problems with the court's mission statement: 'To find a basis for real and substantial agreement

136

through the provision of fast, fair, informal and inexpensive arrangements for the adjudication and resolution of trade disputes.' This statement seemed to me to indicate that the primary role of the court was to fix disputes at all costs, with no reference to the merits or the cost of the claim. To my mind, the mission statement ignores the fundamental requirement to ensure that the cost of any settlement takes into account the interests of all of the parties concerned, not just in the short term but also in the medium and long term.

Resolving disputes is quite simple: all you do is give people what they want. Many people have gained a reputation for being able to resolve disputes but, when the situation is examined carefully, it can be seen that in many instances appeasement rather than resolution was the order of the day.

The measure of a good settlement in any dispute is that all of the parties, having received a fair hearing, get a judgement they can live with, and that the implementation of that judgement does not have long-term negative consequences for the parties.

One of the most challenging aspects of the court is dealing with cases of public significance. While individual cases can give tremendous satisfaction and are vitally important to the people concerned, cases that are of public significance can be time-consuming and stressful. They can require lengthy hearings and a great deal of time and effort in crafting a recommendation for acceptance, in some cases by thousands of workers. Recommendations in the big disputes dealt with by the Labour Court tended to be crafted rather than written, but unfortunately in most instances parties ignore the main points in the recommendation and just go to the last paragraph to see the financial effects it will have. The fact that major parts of the recommendation are ignored usually results in problems arising again within a short space of time.

Public-interest cases can involve issues that affect thousands of people, who are either directly employed or affected by non-resolution of a dispute. In some cases, the claimants feel that, because there are many of them and that, consequently, even a minor movement to resolve their dispute will cost millions, they cannot get justice. From the time I went into the Labour Court, however, I was impressed with the anxiety of everyone involved in the court to ensure that parties had a fair hearing and had every opportunity to put their case and make their arguments. It was always of paramount importance that, by the time individuals left the court, they felt that they had been given every opportunity to make all the arguments they felt were relevant, and that they had given it their best shot.

Even more impressive was the professionalism and concern shown by all the members of the court when considering cases. On occasions, I have been involved in a division that, having come to a particular decision, will, on the basis of a member having agonised overnight, have a change of heart and revise its decision before issuing its recommendation.

The court is very often presented with arguments in relation to the financial situation in a company and asked to make judgements as to whether concession of a claim would in fact be detrimental not just to the company but, in the long term, also to the employees. However, it is frustrating to find that, after a recommendation is issued, recommending deferment of a particular claim because of the financial state of the company, that that same company will subsequently, and often speedily, pay more than was actually sought in the court. This does nothing for the state of industrial relations in Ireland and undermines the credibility of the court. Invariably, the same company will arrive back in the court on another issue, sometimes arguing the same case as before. It is very difficult in those circumstances to take their arguments seriously, as their credibility has been damaged.

On numerous occasions, companies came into the court and argued that to concede a claim would result in disaster for the company. It was therefore no surprise that, when the court decided that there was merit in the case and conceded the claim, the moon didn't fall out of the sky, life went on, and the company continued to make a profit.

Companies frequently argued that business was bad or that the timing of the claim wasn't right and therefore that it should not be conceded at the time. The court, taking into account all of these issues, and agreeing with a company that, due to its financial state at the time, the claim should be put on hold, invariably found that the climate never changed. The company never came back and said that it was in a strong position now, that things were good, and that they wanted to pay some or all of the claim. In fact, the reverse happened in many cases where companies hadn't paid. When the unions or employees went looking for payment of a deferred claim, by the time business had improved the company put forward other reasons why it couldn't pay. One argument was that paying the claim would breach the National Pay Agreement, and another was that 'You could not really count the profits being made as substantial', as it was unlikely that the same level of profits would continue.

One of my earliest experiences in the court was with a particular company that argued forcefully that they would lose market share, become uncompetitive and be forced to cut jobs if they conceded the particular claim. The court took account of this and suggested that the claim be put on hold for twelve months and reviewed at that time. Six weeks later, I got a letter signed by about thirty-five employees saying that I was 'a complete gobshite' and that the company had conned the court. In the end, the employees, having rejected the recommendation and served strike notice, ended up with nearly three times what they had claimed in the court.

The unions, on the other hand, have in many cases taken a very negative view in relation to change and have often asked the court to get the company to guarantee that, if they went along with a particular change, that would be the end of it and there would be no further change. I found this baffling; I often said to the workers' representatives that I could not understand their position because the future for any company that does not change, or does not review its position, is bleak. The issue should be how change is managed. In these cases, the employees were extremely lucky that the management team was at least examining what needed to be done in order to ensure the future of the company.

Another strange phenomenon arose during the height of the Celtic Tiger period, when the court was frequently confronted by unions insisting that more employees should be made redundant than the company had proposed. In effect, the unions were asking us to declare people redundant unnecessarily. Presumably, the availability of jobs made it attractive for people to be made redundant, to get severance pay and find a new job elsewhere.

The description of the Labour Court as 'the court of last resort' has always caused some debate, with some arguing that this applies only for some groups and not for others. Over the years, where groups were able to put pressure on politicians or to cause disruption for the public by going on strike following rejection of a Labour Court recommendation, interventions by a local TD or Minister with the aim of getting a 'white knight' to come in and resolve the problem have undermined this view of the court. Very often in these situations, a Minister, a company or a politician would merely instruct the white knight to fix the dispute regardless of cost, without taking into account the consequences of this course of action for a particular organisation or for an industry as a whole in the longer term.

In order to strengthen the idea of the Labour Court being a court of last resort, one of the first things we did following the project review was to discontinue the revolving-door system which had crept into the process over the years. This arose where, recommendations having been rejected, the parties somehow ended up back at the Labour Relations Commission. By agreement with the commission, a formula was put in place by which the agreement of the court was required before a case that had been heard by the court could go back to the Labour Relations Commission and that this would happen only in rare cases. This agreement was of major significance in that it prevented the practice of another level of appeal being put in place after a hearing by the court.

This policy raised major difficulties at times for some people. Strangely enough, it was the people in union and management circles who should have been supporting the court who often did all in their power to break it. On occasions, the impression was given by the warring parties that it was the Labour Court that was the problem, and that if only the issue had been allowed to be returned to the Labour Relations Commission, the problem would be resolved.

While most parties using the court adhered to the agreements that had been drawn up for normal industrial relations, there is no doubt that, at one stage during the life span of the national pay agreements, certain union officials, during local negotiations, decided to push the case through the Labour Relations Commission and the Labour Court as quickly as possible and get on with the confrontation. Some were extremely successful for their members in this practice, gaining increases over and above the national agreements. Indeed, at one stage, it appeared that those trade union officials who were abiding by the rules were, in fact, disadvantaging their members. This situation was particularly unhelpful when it came to maintaining good industrial relations. It resulted in the discrediting of not just the agreements but also of those who found ways of rewarding such bad behaviour.

It has always been my contention that a claim before the Labour Court must stand on its merits and should not be judged by the amount of damage that could be inflicted by claimants on the company, the public or the government. To operate otherwise is a recipe for anarchy. Over the years, we have seen many examples of individuals and groups using their power to exert pressure with the aim of having their claims met.

The failure to allow management in various areas of the public sector to act as managers, within guidelines, has resulted in settlements that have cost the State more than they might have, had the relevant management people been allowed to do their jobs. One example of this situation was the arguments over payment for working over the new year in the millennium year – the so-called millennium payment. In July or August 1999, this problem could have been put to bed for between £100 and £200 for those public servants who were working at midnight on 31 December 1999. Because a decision was taken by the Department of Finance that there would be no extra payment for people working during this period, this became a major issue for the unions involved. In the long run, it cost the State a lot more money than it would have if the issue had been negotiated at that time rather than at the end of the year, up against a deadline.

In my last few years in the court, in cases involving the Department of Health and Children and the Department of Education, somebody from the Department of Finance has attended the hearing, presumably riding shotgun and overseeing the proceedings. It was never clear whether they were active participants or were merely there to ensure that everybody toed the line. In these circumstances, I always felt it appropriate to address a question to the Department of Finance representative. I took the view that, if someone from this Department was present, any discussion with him or her was part of the court hearing.

Over the years, the court was perceived by many as being aloof, remaining up on the fourth floor of Tom Johnston House in regal splendour. I think this came about from the court's decision over the years never to explain its decisions. This was probably the correct position for the court over the years since its formation in 1946.

The advances that have been made in relation to technology in recent years, with instant and constant media coverage and deadlines, made it necessary to review this policy, particularly with regard to the major cases. It became clear that, if the court maintained this position, there was a danger that the media could, and would, misinterpret the court's recommendations. My predecessor, Evelyn Owens, had greatly enhanced the profile of the court and was prepared to comment on cases, without ever breaching confidentiality or in any way prejudicing the judgements. She was quite willing to tackle the media when necessary.

During this time, a number of highly skilled industrial correspondents had come to the fore – Padraig Yeates of the Irish Times, Tim Hastings of the Irish Independent, Peter Cluskey of RTÉ – and dominated the industrial-relations scene on the media side. In addition, the magazine *Industrial Relations News*, which, then as now, covered all the industrial-relations issues and analysed the performance of the various bodies that dealt with industrial relations – the Employment Appeals Tribunal, the Labour Relations Commission and the Labour Court – made a major impact in this area. The magazine has always been very astute in its assessments and has reported accurately.

During my time as chairman of the Labour Court, the media began to play an increasingly important role in industrial disputes, and it often had a significant influence on the success or failure of proposals to resolve disputes. The input of individuals on *Morning Ireland,* the *News at One* or the six or nine o'clock TV news could often influence the voting pattern of those who were considering a recommendation from the court. For instance, a report in the media prior to a ballot, indicating that a recommendation was likely to be accepted by a particular workforce, often ensured that a significant number voted against it!

Inaccurate analysis of recommendations could also be extremely damaging. Early on in my role as chairman, I experienced a situation where a recommendation went out which was detailed and complex and was reported in a section of the media as having no benefits to the claimants, when in fact the reverse was the case. The damage was done, however: many employees decided to vote against the recommendation on this incorrect analysis.

There is no doubt that the reporting by the media of industrial disputes can have a major effect on the outcome of such disputes. If experienced industrial-relations correspondents are not present, ill-informed judgements can end up being made, and careless assessments of detailed court recommendations can have disastrous effects.

I made it clear to the media, to employers and to trade-union officials that I had no problem with them ringing me up to clarify recommendations, or to give me information that was relevant to any current case, provided that this information could be made available to the other side in the dispute.

During lengthy hearings – a case could go on all day and, in some cases, into the night – it was sometimes difficult to assess what was going on in the minds of the parties. The parties would often go on television or radio, however, and give interviews which would provide indicators as to their thinking; these indicators could be quite helpful when hearing the case. The first thing I did on becoming chairman was to request a television for my office so that, during court recesses, we could watch the six or nine o'clock news and see the parties giving interviews on the court steps. Very few of those who came to the court were camera-shy; in fact, most were only too willing to state their positions on television.

The fact that the court sat late into the night in difficult disputes seemed to impress not only the media but also those involved. Recommendations made following these marathon sessions often had a better chance of being accepted: people were always impressed by late-night sessions.

Over my years in the court, I was involved in very many interesting cases, some involving individuals, others involving groups; many of these cases have left a lasting impression on me. One thing I discovered, however, is that, in many cases, the more educated people are, the more talented they are at writing abusive letters! Some of the abusive letters that I received during the nurses' and teachers' strikes left me in no doubt what some people thought of both me personally and the Labour Court!

One trade-union leader, a man I had great admiration for, gave vent to his feelings about the Court after one of his cases as follows:

Dear Mr Flood,
    I got a short note from poor Mr — expressing his disappointment at the content of the Labour Court

Recommendation in respect of our dispute with — , and asking me what I was going to do next. Union officials are frequently asked such questions, there is very little options [*sic*] or choice in this matter. I could of course burn the edifice down, but that wouldn't help, as the operation would be simply transferred to another location, so instead of doing that, I wrote poor — a short letter. Copy enclosed, which is self-explanatory and which isn't of much help to poor — , but at least I feel a little better. Don't bother replying.

Yours sincerely,


Dear Sir & Brother,

Thank you for your letter 16th July 1997, in which you stated that you were disappointed at the Labour Court Recommendation. I was of the view that we had beaten — 'hands down', and particularly against the background of the letter I had forwarded to the court after the hearing, which was in direct contradiction, and of course factual [*sic*], against some of the statements made by the company in the Labour Court. I was appalled at the Labour Court Recommendation, but not surprised, it's long since a derelict as far as I am concerned, but it is all we have at this point in time.

In 1974, at the Galway ICTU Annual Conference, I had a motion condemning the Labour Court, criticising it for its bad recommendations, the delays in getting into the court, and delays in getting recommendations. At that conference, I did a radio interview with Pat Sweeney of RTÉ confirming my criticism.

I put another motion in, approximately ten years later [in] 1984, again criticising the court. I placed protest pickets on the court on at least three occasions. For the record, I am the only trade-union official in this State, dead or alive, who has engaged in all of these activities against the Labour Court.

I am a voice in the wilderness, a modern-day John the Baptist, without the dancing girls, and unlike poor John, I kept my head in spite of a number of efforts to have it off! The general comment from many other areas of the trade-union movement when I start these anti-establishment campaigns or crusades is 'There goes — again . . . '

The Labour Court needs to be restructured and its duties redefined. The only way to make the proposed changes is, in my view anyway, that all the ICTU Groups of Unions should put a vote of no confidence in the Labour Court and convey that no-confidence vote to Peter Cassells, general secretary of the ICTU and for the attention of the executive council of the ICTU.

Yours fraternally,

PS When I referred to 'having it off', I am of course referring to my head!

This union official gave me my first lesson in negotiation when, as a young manager in the Personnel Department, I refused to move on a particular issue. He told me that leaving the other side nowhere to go in a negotiation would have the same effect as trapping a rat in a corner. 'If you leave me with nowhere to go, I'll have to go through you, just like a rat would,' he said.

From time to time, my wife Anne came with me as I travelled around the country. This suited me very well, as I hate driving and she loves it. It suited her because these trips gave her a chance to see somewhere new or to visit a friend or relation. Once or twice, I took a day's leave and we made a mini-break out of it.

One such occasion was when the court was working in Donegal. Anne was born in Sligo and had known many places close to there, but jumped at the chance to visit Donegal, where she hadn't been for many years. Because we were taking a little break, we booked into Harvey's Point Hotel – which, I hasten to add, was not where the Labour Court personnel were staying! – for a few days.

When we arrived and duly checked in, we were shown to our room, which was apart from the hotel, in a block of rooms in a wooded area. When the porter left the room, Anne said that she was sure the receptionist had called me 'Judge'. I said that she must be imagining it, and we thought no more of it.

That evening, we had our meal in the hotel dining room. We were shown to a lovely table, in a bay window, overlooking the lake. The food and service were both excellent, and we relaxed after our long drive – and a day spent working in Sligo on the way. As we passed the reception desk, we were both sure we heard the receptionist say: 'Goodnight, Judge.' Having had a gin and tonic or two, Anne got a fit of the giggles and thought that this was hilarious.

We were no sooner back in the room than the phone rang. It was the reception desk asking if they should send for the security. I thought this was somebody from the Labour Court playing a joke, probably because we had chosen to stay in a different hotel to the other Labour Court personnel! In spite of my outburst of laughter, the voice at the other end of the phone persisted that, if I had retired for the night, he would send for the Gardaí! I can only assume that I had been mistaken for the then Criminal Court Judge Fergus Flood. I responded that I could sack or reinstate people but that, as this was the limit of my powers, I did not think that I would need the Garda presence! I asked them to cancel the arrangement.

As we laughed at the incident, I suddenly got a cold shiver up my spine: what if any subversives had heard that Justice Flood was staying in Harvey's Point and, in a case of mistaken identity, we were blown to pieces during the night! The laughter stopped then, and we had a very sleepless night.

Still sure that the Labour Court pranksters had been behind this, on my return I told them that there would be a bill coming in from the Gardaí for the overnight presence at the hotel. From their reactions I knew that it had been a genuine case of confusion, and that they had not caused it!

The first case I heard on joining the court related to a young lad who had been working in a late-night restaurant when the owner came in looking for a meal and asked for ketchup. The press containing the ketchup was locked, and the chef had taken home the keys. He explained that he couldn't provide tomato ketchup. The next day, he was told by his manageress that he was no longer required, but he was given no explanation as to why he was being sacked. The lad appeared in the court with his mother and father; their main objective was that they wanted his name cleared. I was quite taken aback that this could have happened. I suppose that, with my background in Guinness, I naively thought that employers generally looked after their employees.

Some months later, while talking to Phil Flynn, the president of ICTU at the time, about some of the cases I had dealt with, he told me that he was delighted when he had heard that I was going into the court. His reasoning was that, coming from a good company like Guinness, I would expect all employers to act as we in the Brewery had.

My second case was in relation to a young lad who had driven a forklift truck at lunchtime and run it into a wall. The trade-union official representing him was not pleading that he had not done what he was charged with but that the area in which he lived was one of high unemployment and that, if he was sacked, the chances of his ever working again were slim.

This young lad was timid-looking; he sat quietly facing the management team, which comprised the managing director, the personnel director and the production director, all in their pin-stripe suits. The management explained that the lad had taken the forklift and had done a lot of damage by running it into a wall. He had been seen by one of them and had been suspended on the spot, pending an investigation. After the submissions had been made outlining the various positions, and before concluding, I asked the young lad if he agreed with what had been said by management and whether they had in fact approached him and talked to him about what he had done. He replied that it had not been as civilised as that at all. His version was that 'Your man got me by the scruff of the neck yelling "If you're not f–ing well out of the place in two minutes I'll break your f–ing neck", and he ran me out the gate.' The whole atmosphere in the court changed: you could see that the young lad, having at this stage accepted that he was not going to be re-employed, got great satisfaction from exploding the myth of the nice management team which had projected themselves as being so polite and reasonable.

In the first month I dealt with a case involving the Dublin Undertakers and learned that there was more to undertaking than moving bodies. Disputes about overtime, lunch allowances and all the normal industrial-relations issues existed even in the world of the dead!

I dealt with a number of sexual-harassment cases – none of which I enjoyed hearing. Such cases are extremely difficult: they are emotional, traumatic and quite stressful for everyone involved, and must be handled in a most sensitive manner by the court. In these cases, I would normally have everybody involved in the case swear on the Bible before giving evidence. Our experience in the court, however, has been that, despite this, completely conflicting evidence is sometimes given by the parties. While it is reasonable that there could be some confusion, given the divergence of evidence in many instances, it is not unreasonable to conclude that one or other of the parties is lying. My fellow court members on several occasions queried my issuing of the oath, saying that it made no difference. I always believed that it did have an effect on some, however, and if it didn't it may be that 'someone would burn for a while in the next life'.

Given that sexual harassment usually occurs between two people in a one-to-one situation, with no witnesses around, it is difficult to decide the merits of the argument. These particular cases sometimes went on for three or four days, depending on the number of witnesses who were called. The court over the years has been concerned that, particularly where an employee takes a case against a member of management, the company will fund the legal expenses of the respondent, whereas the claimant, if he or she employs legal advice, must cover their own costs. The longer the case goes on, however, the more the claimant is eating into any award, because the court does not have the facility to award legal expenses.

On a number of occasions, I have raised with the legislators the possibility of the court being given the facility, where it believes the case is being dragged on unnecessarily, to award legal fees to the claimant. In the present circumstances, claimants can be forced into accepting a settlement on less favourable terms than they feel is fair because, having employed legal representation, they cannot afford to continue with the case.

One of the most pleasing moments I had while chairman of the court was in a pub one evening, when a lady whom I recognised as having been involved in a sexual-harassment case came over to me and thanked me for the sensitive manner in which I had conducted the case. I was extremely pleased that, with all the stress and strain she had undergone, she believed she had been treated fairly and with dignity and consideration by the court.

The nurses' dispute in 1999 was probably my highest-profile case, given the numbers involved and the effect the dispute had on the country. My predecessor, Evelyn Owens, had issued a recommendation two years earlier on nurses' pay and conditions; elements of this recommendation that were still outstanding came back to the court. As a result, we issued a follow-up recommendation. This was rejected, and the nurses went on strike. Subsequently, we had another hearing and, after discussions had taken place in Government Buildings, we produced another recommendation – which was accepted by the nurses. The usual abusive letters arrived during this dispute. One such letter read:

Dear Sir,

I wrote to you at the beginning of summer, and I believe I left you in no doubt as to what my feelings were towards the Labour Court and your judgement.

Given the findings of the Commission on Nursing, given your previous rulings and the reaction to same, I hold the view that you should be ashamed of yourself to put your name to the document of 27/10/99. Like politicians, most of you get where you are by having a neck like a jockey's bollocks, and having studied this document I can only conclude you have that neck.

In my view Ahern is still signing blank cheques.

Do the honourable thing – resign.

Independent Labour Court – independent my arse.

The teachers' dispute was also a major one and was particularly acrimonious. The teachers' union ASTI, having decided to stay outside the national pay agreement and benchmarking, was looking for a 30 percent increase in pay. We were asked to hear their case, even though, technically, they were not entitled to come to the court.

During the afternoon session, we became conscious that the atmosphere had changed, but we couldn't understand why this had happened. During a recess, we decided to watch the six o'clock news to see what their take on the situation was. Sure enough, we discovered, to our amazement, that, during the same period that they had been talking to us, ASTI had voted for a one-day strike, to take place the next day. Needless to say, we were appalled at this and we subsequently cancelled all talks until the teachers called off their strike. They claimed that they had people all over the country and they couldn't get them back, but we were insistent that this was their problem and that, unless they called off their action, we would call off the talks.

A major casualty that night was my tea. We had ordered fish and chips from the local chipper. When I heard the ASTI representatives saying that they were going on strike, I was so outraged that I threw the chips up in the air and lost them all. While

I tried to persuade my colleagues to go back down immediately to the court and confront the ASTI, they refused to do so until they had finished their fish and chips! My short fuse cost me my tea!

During the ASTI strike, it was brought to my notice that the Education Committee of the Dáil was in session and was berating the Labour Court over its recommendation and requesting that the Court change its recommendation. Worse still, one member appeared to indicate that there was no sense in going back to the court, as he had spoken to the court and knew its views on the matter.

Having watched the video of the committee's proceedings, I was shocked. I immediately phoned the TD who had indicated that he had spoken to the court. He initially stated that he had not said that he had contacted the court. When I explained to him that I had watched it on video and left him in no doubt as to how damaging his statement was for the independence of the court, he said that he had been misunderstood. Subsequently, I wrote to the committee emphasising that the Labour Court was an independent statutory body and that they obviously had not understood the background to the dispute.

It has always surprised me how poorly some management teams read the signs in disputes. In one particular dispute, where the recommendation had been rejected, the management believed from information that they had been given that, if an extra penny was put on the rate for the top grade, it would give people a chance to ballot again and 'get off the hook'. Despite the fact that I did not believe there was an earthly chance of this running, I was told that management was confident that the strike would be rescinded and that the problem would be resolved.

To indicate how out of touch this company had become, when the ballot subsequently came through, there were eighty votes against the new proposal and none in favour of it. It is fair to say that, in this particular case, management got it wrong. In addition, the company subsequently ended up paying far more than they might have if they had gone about things in the right way and made a realistic offer to resolve the dispute in the first instance.

Working in multinational companies brings its own stresses, as there is always tension between the centre and the outposts. Managers need to learn special skills because the piranhas at head office can take the flesh off you before you even get into the water! Frequently in the Labour Court I was conscious that the managers of such operations were trying to paint a positive picture of progress back to HQ, in Europe or the USA, when in fact the outlook was anything but positive.

In some such cases, while the issue before the Court appeared to be relatively minor, it was clear that it would colour HQ's view of the Irish operation, with serious medium-term consequences for that operation. Employees find it hard to accept that someone in Europe or the USA can wipe an operation off the corporate map without even being sure where it is located!

Over the years, the number of health and education disputes coming before the court has increased significantly. In some situations, the court was informed that management was supportive of the claim, or at worst was not opposed to it, but that the Department of Finance would not agree to its being conceded. This resulted in the court's time and efforts being wasted. The court was thus being used to get the 'Harp' on the recommendation so that the Department of Finance would have to concede the claim. Such issues should be sorted out within government and not in the Labour Court. The Department of Finance must keep an eye on the public purse, but it must do so in such a way that the cost to the public does not increase. In many instances, the approach in these cases does just that: increases the cost. If management was left to its own devices, it is possible that a reasonable compromise would be found. If there is no confidence in the local management, this matter should be addressed – but not, as at present, by making a mockery of the machinery of the State.

During my spell in the court, one thing that annoyed me greatly was the way in which some people in very senior positions tried to put pressure on so that certain cases would be heard as a priority in the court, in situations where the parties involved had behaved very badly. Sometimes, the employees had voted for strike action before going through the relevant procedures; in other cases, companies had refused to engage in any discussions and had then faced the inevitable strike – at which point they decided not only that they wanted to get into discussions but also that they wanted to jump the queue and have their case heard above those who had been abiding by the rules.

While I believe that we have to be pragmatic and ensure that the country does not grind to a halt, this kind of behaviour from people at the top does nothing to encourage the honouring of agreements and respect for the agreed procedures. Unfortunately, we have become a country where bad behaviour at all levels is rewarded.

The pace of change in relation to new technology and globalisation in the marketplace has created new and different industrial-relations challenges. For instance, the court currently hears numerous cases that relate to restructuring and change programmes. These cases can be complex and frequently require detailed examination of the financial structures and performance of companies.

For me, one of the frustrating aspects of the work of the court was its lack of powers to enforce awards. Claimants believed that their awards were automatically guaranteed but frequently found that they had to go to the civil courts for the awards to be enforced. Another matter I found unsatisfactory was the fact that, when making awards, the court was constrained in many instances by the statutory limit of 104 weeks' pay. This was frustrating, particularly in sexual-harassment cases: it often resulted in a claimant being forced to make a settlement before the case had been fully heard, rather than see the legal costs substantially eat into any award. The 104-weeks-pay rule also fails to take account of low wages and can result in the actual amount of the award failing to reflect the gravity of the case.

The chairman of the court must at all times be prepared to speak out if he or she sees something that is damaging to the general management of industrial relations nationally and, more importantly, that affects the operations or image of the court. For that reason, on several occasions I made statements to the press or comments in relation to issues that were in the public domain and were likely to affect the court.


Working in the public sector, as I was during my time in the Labour Court, was a new experience for me. In the private sector, people were by and large rewarded or promoted based on merit alone. I soon became aware, however, that in the civil service there were a number of other ways of being promoted. There was the 'consistory' process – which entailed a group of managers deciding who should be promoted based on seniority and suitability – and the traditional approach, involving an interview or a job-application process. It appeared to me that a significant number of promotions came according to time served rather than ability. When I wanted to put a junior person into a senior post to test their ability, the rules seemed to prevent it. Indeed, the rules often seemed to operate *against* the requirements of the business we were conducting, as well as to the detriment of the development of individual members of staff. In the Labour Court, we had some excellent people who were doing very routine jobs and were capable of much more, but it wasn't possible to give them the opportunity to expand their skills.

Eventually, I came to the conclusion that it was not feasible to bring about the type of change I was looking for, within the timescale of my tenure. Being told 'it can't be done' becomes frustrating. I ultimately got to the stage of saying to people at meetings: 'I know this can't be done, and I know there are reasons why it can't be done, but I just want to know the date on which we will introduce it.'

Most of the people I worked with in the public sector were extremely impressive and capable and were quite capable of doing the job of the person above them. The chances of them getting this opportunity were slim, however, given the nature of the system in which they found themselves.

I was extremely lucky to have had two excellent deputy chairmen of the court. I had known Kevin Duffy for a long time prior to our working together in the court, through his involvement in ICTU and my role in Guinness and, indeed, in IBEC. We had also served together on the board of the Labour Relations Commission when it was set up in 1990. I believe that Kevin will be the best chairman the court has ever had. He has the industrial-relations experience, the legal qualifications and the human touch, and he takes no nonsense from anyone. In fact, one of the things I miss most since retiring from the court is my early-morning cup of coffee and chat with Kevin, when we used to address the problems of the world.

Caroline Jenkinson came in from IBEC with little practical industrial-relations experience but with a wealth of knowledge in terms of labour legislation. She is particularly able and dedicated and undoubtedly has the potential to take over from Kevin as chairman when he decides to hang up his spurs.

When I retired, I felt that, during my time as chairman of the court, I had given some of the younger members of staff a hard time. As a result, I expected that they would be delighted to see the end of me. One of my greatest satisfactions, however, was the send-off I got from the staff, particularly the comments made by various staff members whom I thought would be glad to see the back of me! I have always believed that people should take pride in where they work. Consequently, it was very important to me that the staff of the court got as much satisfaction from the Labour Court successfully resolving a major dispute as the court members did. There was always a good feeling when the court did well, and everyone shared in the success.

For the court to function properly, it must have the support of government, the social partners and all who use it as a means of dispute resolution. It must continually work to maintain its reputation for professionalism, integrity and fair play, earned over a period of sixty years. I hope that, during my ten years in the court, I lived up to the ideals maintained by my predecessors.

4

## A Career in Football

Football kept me sane during the period in my life when my work in the brewery was monotonous and soul-destroying. Luckily, my career at work took off shortly after my career in football finished. While my football career bore little resemblance to those of young footballers today, with their high salaries and glamorous lifestyle, football nevertheless gave me, and many others, huge satisfaction and a purpose in life.

It always amazed me that there were people around who were prepared to pay me money for doing something I loved and would do for nothing. Initially, it felt unnatural to be negotiating payment for playing football, but I quickly got used to it!

Football grounds such as Milltown and Tolka Park were full most Sundays in the fifties and sixties, and supporters who were not at the ground at least fifteen minutes before kick-off risked not gaining entry. There were hundreds of bikes piled along the walls; the bikes' owners paid a penny to a minder for keeping an eye on their property. Special buses were laid on from O'Connell Street to Milltown and Tolka Park.

The game was full of characters: Bunny Fulham, 'Sheila' Darcy and, of course, Ben Hannigan. Bunny was a hard-tackling fullback whose jousts with Liam Tuohy were legendary. Eamon Darcy, or 'Sheila', as he was known, was a spectacular goalkeeper who performed for the crowd, doing tricks while making magnificent saves. Ben Hannigan was a 'performer' in every sense of the word. The rivalry between teams and their supporters was intense but seldom aggressive. In fact, it was a golden era for League of Ireland football because of big crowds, no television and less intrusion from across the water.

One of the advantages of being involved in football during this period was that there were very few other attractions for people. Social life revolved mainly around the football ground, the cinema and the dance hall. The pub culture applied only to another age group. Most of us who grew up during that period look back on those times with great fondness, perhaps viewing the period through rose-tinted glasses. People still stop me, even now, on the street to say: 'I remember you playing in the good old days' – in my case in goal for Shelbourne. Many will recall particular matches and incidents as though they happened yesterday, when in fact it was more than forty years ago. It is strange how, in sport, reputations improve over the years and even people who criticised a particular person in the past now remember him as a great player!

Many sportsmen and women are not conscious during their careers that they have a sell-by date. The adoration they enjoy during their sporting careers will, in most cases, dwindle dramatically once they are no longer at the top of their sport. There is nothing as fickle as the sports fans!

It has always been a source of concern to me that so many sportsmen and women fail to realise how tenuous their careers are if injury strikes. Watching some of the current stars and their arrogance – some of them seem to believe that they can walk on water – I fear for them when they have to retire. In football, we have gone from the era of the maximum wage of £20 to the huge earnings of today, when many top players are multimillionaires, without protecting the more vulnerable against the loneliness and possible poverty of retirement. Most footballers now have financial advisers to protect their cash, whereas in fact many have a greater need to have someone to prepare them psychologically for returning to the real world.

In the early 1990s, I was invited back to one of my former clubs, Morton in Scotland, for a weekend. As my wife Anne and I sat on the plane, I realised that I didn't really know why I was heading back there after all this time. I wondered if anyone would even remember me after twenty years. It then dawned on me that it was actually thirty years, not twenty. Where did the time go?

That trip in 1992 turned out to be a momentous one for me. When I retired from football, due to a major injury in 1967, I thought I had handled it well and accepted the situation. I had always known that it would all come to an end.

When I arrived at Cappielow Park, Morton's ground, however, and was brought into the dressing room to meet the players (one of whom told me that his father had lifted him over the stiles to watch me, the 'Man in Black', play), it all came flooding back to me. The dressing-room banter and the smell of the embrocation – used to warm the legs and prevent pulled muscles – forced me to step out into the corridor, where I was overcome with emotion: the tears flowed. This must have been some type of delayed reaction, thirty years later, but it really brought home to me what I had lost, forever – the camaraderie, the excitement and the anticipation of the roar of the crowd.

As a young professional footballer, without the support of a footballing family, I had to fend for myself and protect myself, particularly when it came to money. Football clubs were not noted for taking care of their young players, and most would wipe your eye every chance they got.

In those days, footballers had no rights and were badly treated by the clubs. In the League of Ireland, if a player displeased his club he could be placed on a 'retained list' forever – meaning that he could not play for another club – and he would not be paid a penny. When I went to play for Holyhead, I played with Shay Nolan (ex-Shelbourne), who had been put out of the game in Ireland after being retained by Shelbourne. This was a vicious practice and destroyed the careers of many footballers.

In the early sixties, Jimmy Hill, who had formed the Players' Union in England, travelled over to Ireland and met with a number of players, notably Shay Keogh and Mick Lynch, and advised on the setting up of a Players' Union in Ireland. A problem arose at the first meeting, however, because the clubs were so powerful that none of the players could run the risk of taking on the post of being chairman of the union. In the end, Alan Glynn – a brother of Dessie Glynn of Drumcondra Football Club and subsequently the chief executive of the Jurys Doyle Hotel Group, offered to put himself forward for chairman.

Although the clubs were making significant sums of money, players were paid only £3 or £4 per week. The wheel has certainly turned full circle: some players in Ireland are now paid €50,000 to €90,000 a year. Clubs such as Bohemians and Shelbourne are now spending nearly €2 million per annum to run the club; gate receipts bring in less than a quarter of the total, with the rest coming from television networks and UEFA prize money.

While the money rolled in, the grounds and the facilities were certainly not up to scratch. When I look at the grounds today, it is clear that most have improved significantly. In the case of Tolka Park, I often remark that in the old days, when the ball hit the grass it was a throw-in, as most of the pitch area was made up of sand. Early in the season, being a goalkeeper, my knees were cut to bits from the sand and had to be bandaged: they would most likely remain like that for the entire season. For one reason or another, goalkeepers did not have the sense to wear tracksuit bottoms; I am not sure if they were allowed then.

Having been persuaded by a woman in a post office in Liverpool, at the age of eleven, that I should play in goal, all my childhood was spent trying to improve my catching skills. I spent many afternoons in Ross Street as a child, banging a ball off a wall and catching it on the rebound. I spent a lot of time trying to imitate Lev Yashin, the Russian goalkeeper, who always wore black and trained in a sandpit to improve his leg strength and jumping skills.

A recent programme on RTÉ about Mick O'Connell, the great Kerry midfielder, showed how he trained endlessly by banging a ball off the gable end of his house. Looking at pictures of him as a young lad, catching the ball, brought back memories of my own days in Ross Street.

During the era when I played in goal, it was legitimate to charge the goalkeeper once he had the ball. The goalkeeper was also limited to taking five steps before kicking the ball out. Part of the entertainment was watching goalkeepers being chased and charged and, in many cases, kicked as they went for the ball. Goalkeepers quickly learned to go up for a ball with their knees up and their elbows out to protect themselves. in fact, many England international goalkeepers had nightmares after playing in Dalymount and being chased around by League of Ireland centre-forwards. The most famous centre-forward–goalkeeper clash was when Nat Lofthouse of Bolton charged Ray Wood, the Manchester United goalkeeper, over the line in Wembley for a goal in the Cup Final, breaking his jaw in the process.

Training dominated my life, to the exclusion of many youthful pleasures. After he had retired from athletics, the great Herb Elliot, the Australian runner, questioned such dedication and the wisdom of giving up so much for sport. Training every Tuesday and Thursday was a must for me, however: I don't think I ever missed a training session. Even if I was injured, I would still make my way to the ground on training nights. We were obviously made of tougher stuff back then!

When I played with Shelbourne, Irishtown stadium was our training ground. It was such a bleak place, with a running track around the football pitch, grey walls, sparse terraces – and very little else. The wind howled there on winter nights; it was tough going. There were no lights, and when we ran around the running track at night, it was possible, if we were knackered, for one or two of us to duck behind the wall, take a breather and join in on the next lap. We had to have our wits about us to make sure there was going to be a next lap to allow us to join in, otherwise we could wind up in big trouble!

Shelbourne had ambitions to develop Irishtown, with the athletics supremo Billy Morton, for athletics and football. This was the great athletics period in Ireland: the era of Brendan O'Reilly, the high jumper; Eamon Kinsella, the Olympic hurdler; and John Joe Barry, the great miler. Unfortunately, things did not work out, and Billy Morton developed Santry Stadium instead.

Our trainer, Dick Hearns, was a former Golden Glove boxer, having boxed against the USA. He had tremendous enthusiasm and a very strong will to win. He could never understand how, when we were on a bonus to win, the opposition even survived to walk off the pitch at the end of the game. He claimed that, if *he* was on a fiver bonus to win a game, none of them would be left standing at the end of the ninety minutes.

Dick often reminisced about his boxing career. He was especially proud of his selection for the Golden Glove team. He often told me that, when he went with the team to America, he was given an allowance but managed to have more money in his pocket when he returned home. He always took great pride in telling me how his home was beautifully furnished from his successful boxing career.

He had his own drink concoction that he mixed for the players, which was referred to as 'jungle juice'. We all took this before a game. I can only wonder what was in it – I assume it was harmless stuff. Today it might be a different story and we could be in big trouble, given that we never enquired as to its content. Jungle juice was essential before every game, and taking it became a ritual for us.

My schoolboy football really started at the age of eleven with Munster Victoria, which was run by Jim Tunney. I played as an inside-forward for them until we went over on an Easter trip to Liverpool, a trip we funded by saving a shilling a week all season. That particular trip was in 1949, when the effects of the war were still being felt around Liverpool. The guesthouse we stayed in fed us with powdered eggs and horse meat; everyone was delighted to get even that much.

I subsequently played in goal for Kirwan Rovers, a team put

together by a man called Jimmy Lynch, who worked in Liptons in Dame Street, and a bus conductor named Maurice Fitzsimons. They financed the team from their own pockets. We only managed to scrape together a set of jerseys by selling coupons for a company in Blessington Street; in return, the company supplied the jerseys. Shorts and socks were entirely another matter. Each individual was expected to get his own – or live in hope that the club might come to his aid and somehow supply them. Our team was not well known like the 'glamour sides', such as Home Farm, Johnville and Stella Maris. We were on the periphery, always struggling, forever hopeful.

During our teenage football years, one of the brewery messengers, Mick White, was spotted by Blackburn Rovers and brought over to England on a regular basis to play in the Youth Cup. This was a first, and it created a huge buzz in Dublin, particularly in the brewery. While nowadays, many young footballers go to England, at that time it had not happened. Mick White did not move to England but subsequently played for Drumcondra.

In 1956, Billy King, who ran Shamrock Rovers Minors, called to my house in Ross Street and asked me to sign for them. This was big-time – Billy King calling to our house! It was probably one of the greatest moments of my life: suddenly I was established, and nothing else seemed to matter. This was the club my Aunt Cathy and I had followed and idolised for years.

At the age of seventeen, I turned up for pre-season training in Milltown full of fear and trepidation. At the start of the season, Paddy Coad had the first team, the second team and the minors all training together. The first-team goalkeeper, Christy O'Callaghan, and the reserve goalkeeper were down at one end, and at the other end, covering the width of the pitch, were myself and a character by the name of Eamon Darcy, who had just returned from Oldham Athletic. That night, during the periods when we didn't have much to do, Eamon bombarded me with questions: how good was Christy O'Callaghan and how long had he been the first-team goalkeeper. This particular night heralded the entrance of Eamon, one of the greatest characters ever to play the game, to League of Ireland football. Eamon was a tremendous asset to Shamrock Rovers and the League for many seasons.

For me, playing for Shamrock Rovers, even for the Minors team, was the equivalent of playing for Manchester United in the Premier League. Minor players with Rovers were treated like the first and second teams, so all our kit was supplied, right down to our boots. Wherever we played, these were handed to us clean from the team skip. We created a major stir wherever we played. You can imagine the faces of the smaller schoolboy clubs' players, and how they felt when we arrived to play with our skip carried in as though we were full-time professionals!

In very small grounds, such as Broombridge in Cabra, we always made a point of running on to the pitch together like a professional team. We were immaculately turned out and, as a result, psychologically started a goal up. On this particular Minors team, three of the players were already professionals, even though they were under eighteen. They were being paid professional wages — something that was unheard of at that time.

During my period in Milltown as a Minor, I got to see Paddy Coad in action, coaching and training his players. He was ahead of his time in terms of tactics and thought processes – the greatest player ever to play in the League of Ireland, in my opinion. At that time, Paddy Coad had put together the best-ever League of Ireland side. It included such greats as Gerry Mackey, Liam Hennessey, Liam Tuohy, Paddy Ambrose, Mick Burke, Christy O'Callaghan, Tommy Hamilton and himself. Their memory lives on among those who were lucky enough to have seen them in action or to have played against them. I had the pleasure of seeing them in Dalymount Park playing the Busby Babes: Duncan Edwards, Roger Byrne, Tommy Taylor and of course Liam Whelan. Although they got hammered that night, they were still the best team that ever played in the League of Ireland.

My time with Shamrock Rovers Minors probably gave me the confidence to overcome the inferiority complex I had suffered throughout my teenage years. When you played for Shamrock Rovers, even the Minors, you believed you were somebody special.

In those days, football followers took a particular interest in the English clubs that had Irish players on their books. The fortunes of the clubs that people like Charlie Hurley and Noel Cantwell played for were followed enthusiastically. When Paddy Turner and I headed over to play for Morton Football Club in Scotland, Morton suddenly had a fan base of people who had never even heard of Morton Football Club before then. I still meet people who throw their eye over Morton's results because they started to follow the club when Paddy and I were with them. When *Sports Report* on the BBC started, everyone the length and breadth of the country tuned in at 5 o'clock on a Saturday evening.

The Shamrock Rovers Minors Team of 1958 was made up of the best players in Dublin, recruited by Billy King, including Harry Lennon, Bobby Gilbert and Paddy Turner. It won the AUL League and Cup and was expected to win everything. Unfortunately, we missed out on the biggest prize of all, the FAI Minor Cup, going down 2–1 in the semi-final to Athlone in Tolka Park, in a game we should never have lost. If memory serves me correctly, I had only a few shots to save in that game, and two hit the net. It was probably my first major disappointment in sport. I blamed myself for the defeat and spent that Sunday afternoon in the Cabra Grand Cinema, trying to hide from reality. It was a tremendous pity that we lost the Cup that year, because in the two subsequent years I was to win FAI Junior and Senior Cup medals. I would have won Minor, Junior and Senior medals in consecutive years – a record that would have been hard to beat.

Following my time with Shamrock Rovers, I went over to play in a trial match with Holyhead Town in the Welsh League. A number of Irish players travelled over on the 'mail boat' every Friday night and returned on the 3 AM boat on Sunday morning. Jim Farmer, who had been the Shelbourne goalkeeper up to that year, also attended for trial, and he was signed by Holyhead.

I didn't make it onto the Holyhead team and instead went to play for Virginians, who were connected to the Players tobacco factory in Glasnevin in Dublin. The Virginians Club had a very enthusiastic committee; dances were held on several Saturdays throughout the year in the clubhouse in Glasnevin. It was a very social kind of club.

In the summer, the soccer pitch was turned into a cricket pitch – much to the disgust of some of the cricket teams. Many a cricket match was won and lost due to the bumps and hollows on that pitch. Most junior cricket teams that came to play there complained bitterly about the poor standard of the pitch. It made no difference to us, though: we were delighted to win against the more snobby, well-to-do clubs.

The event that gave me the greatest satisfaction in my sporting life happened during my time at Virginians. This was winning the mile in the Players Tobacco Sports in 1959. Even though I was one of the fittest players in the club, I trained obsessively for these sports, and the work paid off. I was also on the winning team in the relay. These events showed me the difference between winning a team event and the personal satisfaction of achieving something on your own. When I won the mile, I can clearly remember seeing one runner ahead of me and knowing that I was going to catch him. I just knew that nothing was going to stop me. It was an amazing feeling. When I heard Eamonn Coughlan talking about passing the Russian athlete in the World Championships, I knew exactly how he felt!

We trained very hard for Virginians in the 1958–59 season. The team had been beaten in the FA Junior Cup Final by Glenmore Celtic the year before, and we were determined that nothing would stand in the way of us winning the Cup this time. Halfway through the season, as we arrived to train one night, we heard about the Munich air crash. We all sat around the radio listening to the tragic news. It was probably the first big tragedy I had experienced. We all felt we knew the Busby Babes. We had shared in their success from afar, given the involvement of Liam

Whelan from Cabra. We were devastated and, probably for the first time in our lives, realised how fickle life can be.

In the quarter-finals of the Junior Cup, held on St Patrick's Day, while playing Ballynanty Rovers in Limerick, I received a kick to the head, which resulted in a broken nose and cheekbone. I was carried off the pitch but travelled back by train with the players, and played poker all the way back! Nobody realised exactly how bad I was until I collapsed as I walked out of the station in Kingsbridge. The pain got worse, and two days later, when it became unbearable, I was rushed by ambulance to the Richmond Hospital. The doctors there discovered the seriousness of the injury: I had a laceration of the brain. I spent many weeks in hospital; in the bed opposite was a close friend of mine from the brewery, Willie Doyle. He had broken his neck playing rugby on the same day I had sustained my head injury. Neither of us could sleep, and we spent many nights chatting through the night. We promised God during that time that if we got through this ordeal we would never again complain about having to work the 6 AM shift at the brewery – or indeed anything else in life.

It was many months before I returned to football. Jim Kevlin, a centr-half with Virginians, replaced me in goal. He had to adapt to his new position, as he was not a recognised goalkeeper. By the time we reached the final in Dalymount, the selectors decided that I should play in the final.

At this stage, I felt I was ready to go back, but on the day of the Junior Cup Final, standing outside the church in Phibsboro with Kevin Nugent, one of the selectors, my nerve began to go, and I started to question whether it was a good idea for me to play. If I was expecting any sympathy, I was in for a rude awakening! He immediately retorted: 'If you don't want to be here, go home, and stop wasting my time. We have to get on with it.' Looking back on it, this was a turning point: if I had not gone on to play that day, I might never have played again. We went on to win the Cup Final, beating Swilly Rovers from Donegal 3–1.

Between the trials for Holyhead and playing for Virginians, I had played five matches for Sligo Rovers. (The rules allowed a player to play five matches in the League of Ireland before losing his junior status and no longer being eligible to play in the Junior Cup.) The first of the matches I played for Sligo at eighteen was against the great Shamrock Rovers side at the Showgrounds. Although we were beaten 2–0 on the day, the club was extremely satisfied with my performance and I played a further four matches.

One of these matches, against Drumcondra in Tolka Park, sticks out in my mind, as we were beaten 5–1. My disappointment following this defeat was not helped by W. P. Murphy – who was nicknamed 'Waste Paper', and was one of the best soccer reporters – poking his head around the dressing-room door to enquire if I had actually scored Drumcondra's last goal myself. Not very sensitive!

After we won the FA Junior Cup, Holyhead approached me. They said they had made a mistake in not signing me the previous year and asked me to sign for them. I decided to sign, and began to travel back and forth to Holyhead by boat each weekend.

Travelling to Holyhead then was primitive: it could be a horrendous journey. By the time the football season settled down in October or November, the *Hibernia* and other reputable ships had been taken off the route to be overhauled. They were replaced by the *Princess Maud,* which, given the amount of water it took on board, was more like a submarine than a boat. There always seemed to be water pouring over the sides onto the decks and into the lounges. The lounges had wooden battens in the floors for the cattle the ship normally carried. A luxury liner it was not!

Although going to and from Holyhead could be difficult from the point of view of travelling it was exciting at the same time. To be getting paid for playing football, in a foreign country, was a great adventure for a nineteen-year-old. The pay was about £4 per game, and three of us – Paddy Kearns, Archie Grimes and I – made the journey every week, while other players, like John Kavanagh and Sonny Rice, travelled over to play for other Welsh teams. This was an era when Mars Bars and Wilkinson Sword Edge blades were unavailable in Ireland, so we brought back stocks of them every Sunday morning.

I was still working away in the brewery. Juggling my job and my football career wasn't too difficult, given that my job was going nowhere. Also, by a stroke of good fortune, the five-day working week was introduced in the brewery the week I signed for Holyhead

At this time, I was beginning to get shrewd. I was inclined to watch what was happening in various clubs, with a view to anticipating where the next opportunity might arise. Given that there were only twelve League of Ireland clubs, there were very few opportunities for goalkeepers.

I had noticed that Shelbourne had not been doing well in the Shield competitions at the start of the season. Experience had taught me that clubs on the bottom rung of the ladder at this early stage of the season usually changed their goalkeeper before the league started, so I wasn't too surprised when Shelbourne approached me.

Gerry Doyle was the manager of Shels at that time, and he had built a very young side from St Finbarr's Schoolboys. He had available to him a host of young players, including Eric Barber, Jackie Hennessey and Tony Dunne, who went on to play for Manchester United. After he approached me, I signed for the club on a Thursday night in my family home in Manor Street, with Saturday's date on the form. Holyhead had insisted that I travel over to play for them in a Cup match against Wrexham that Saturday.

On my last trip to Holyhead, the *Princess Maud* hit a storm. We took six and a half hours to reach Holyhead, eventually pulling into port at 3.30 in the morning. Every window in the lounge had been broken, and armchairs had been flying through the air. I was glad it was my last trip on that boat. I returned on Sunday morning at 7 AM and immediately travelled to Cork to play against Hibernians.

I had an understanding with Shelbourne that, if I held my

place on the first team for four consecutive matches, I would be entitled to more money than I had originally signed for. My first business lesson came as a result of this agreement, when, on the Sunday night after we had drawn with Hibernians in Cork, I raised this agreement with the club in the Cahir Hotel. They informed me that what was in my contract was what I would be paid. I quickly learned that market forces must be exploited at their peak, otherwise they have no value. The other lesson I learned for the future was to have everything in writing. Needless to say, I never did get the increase I expected.

That match in Cork was the first match played by Charlie Tully, who had signed for Hibernians from Glasgow Celtic. We drew 1–1 and went on to have quite a successful season, winning the FAI Cup in April 1961, beating Cork Hibernians 2-0.

The Shelbourne side that I joined was a great one, with enormous potential. Most of the players were around twenty years of age. The regular line-out was Flood, Tony Dunne, O'Brien, Theo Dunne, Strahan, Kelly, Wilson, Hennessy, Barber, Doyle, Conroy.

We played Shamrock Rovers on the way to the final that year. I went to see them play in Milltown the week before we played them in the Cup. At the end of the match, I vaulted over the wall to make a quick exit from the ground. I fell on my wrist and sprained it, and as a result, I missed the Cup match the following Sunday. Rovers finished that game with only nine men, after Gerry Mackey and Liam Hennessey collided and had to be stretchered off.

In those days, substitutes were not allowed, but the nine Rovers men held Shelbourne to a 1–1 draw. Bookies were offering odds of 4 to 1 against Shelbourne winning the replay. A lot of the dockers in Ringsend took the odds and cleaned up. We beat Rovers 3–0 that night, with Christy Doyle hitting the back of the net with a brilliant header.

In the Cup semi-final against Dundalk in Dalymount, during the first half I sustained a kick to the hand from Jimmy Hasty (the one-armed Dundalk player). During half-time, our trainer examined me and said that my fingers, still in woollen gloves,

171

were dislocated. He proceeded to pull my fingers back into place. I went out and finished the game, which we won 4–1. Unfortunately, my three fingers were broken, not dislocated, and once again I was out of the game for a few weeks.

As if to prove how large a part luck plays in life, Billy Behan, the reserve goalkeeper, who would have played in the Cup Final in my absence, sustained a kick to his back in a match in Cork just before the final. As he was unable to play, it was decided that I would play with my three broken fingers heavily strapped.

The Cup Final was an uneventful match, with Shelbourne winning 2–0. Cork spent much of the first half trying to get a kick at my broken fingers – or so it seemed to me. This was the practice of the day: when teams found a weakness, they went for it both physically and psychologically. But my hand and I somehow survived the day. That match was Tony Dunne's last for Shelbourne: he signed for Manchester United that night and went on to have a great career.

When I see how players are looked after today, I realise how badly we were treated. There was no dinner to celebrate our Cup victory, and no question of girlfriends or wives being included in the after-match celebrations. Instead, the players adjourned to the Gresham Hotel immediately after the game for sandwiches and a cake – thanks to Paddy Roberts, who was a chef there and who also played for Shelbourne. That night I was tucked up in bed at home by half-past ten, with a feeling of bitter disappointment about the non-existent celebrations. It was a huge anticlimax.

The European Cup Final of 1960 was played in Hampden Park between Real Madrid and Eintracht. It turned out to be a classic, remembered to this day, with Real Madrid winning 7–3. After the final, it was widely reported that Real Madrid were coming to play Shelbourne. This generated great excitement in Dublin, and the players looked forward to the match with a mixture of fear and anticipation. In any case, the thought of facing the banana shot – something we had never seen before – was daunting. Unfortunately, the game never materialised.

When I signed for Shelbourne from Holyhead, I was paid four pounds and ten shillings per week. I later discovered – at a meeting held by the players at the Imperial Hotel in Sligo to look for a pay rise at the start of the 1961–62 season – that this was ten shillings more than the rest of the team were being paid.

At the meeting, the players felt that their efforts were not being rewarded by the club. It was decided by everyone to seek an extra pound in our wages. This, it was said, would bring everyone up from £4 to £5. Unfortunately, I was left with a dilemma: should I keep the fact that I was receiving ten shillings more than the rest of them to myself or acknowledge it. I decided that honesty was the best policy and told everyone that I was in fact receiving the ten shillings more. Not surprisingly, this caused consternation: as well as looking for the additional pound raise, some players were asking why I should be receiving more to begin with.

It was pointless trying to explain that, when I had come from Holyhead, Shelbourne were in need of a goalkeeper and therefore willing to pay a little extra. I was afraid to tell them that the original agreement was for me to be paid £6 if I held my place for four consecutive matches but that this had been reneged on!

When the claim was made for the one-pound rise, the club called me into the boardroom and blamed me for creating the uproar. The view was that, if I had kept my mouth shut, the problem would not have emerged in the first place. Despite the fact that this was untrue, when the others were eventually awarded the extra pound, I got only ten shillings extra. We all ended up on the same money – a fiver a week – at least I *think* we were all then on the same money!

Every year, when renegotiating our individual contracts with the club, we had to be alert and examine carefully what we were signing. Even slight changes in the wording could lead to a significant difference in our financial package. Terms such as that we were to be paid £5, say, 'when playing' meant that a player who was unlucky enough to be injured or not on the first team would not be paid that amount. The young and uninitiated easily fell into this trap – and only discovered later that it was hard to get out of. Just as I had found out, 48 hours after signing from Holyhead, that the verbal agreement I had with the club was worthless, omissions from the contract would not subsequently be included.

In those days, players had no rights, and many were treated badly. Some were retained by clubs for years and paid nothing: they were inevitably being put out of the game. The Players Union was formed to protect players and to discontinue the practice of clubs retaining players while not paying them.

Just as I had been called into the boardroom about disclosing the fact that I was being paid ten shillings more than the other players, I had another experience of being summoned to the boardroom early in the 1961–62 season. This followed the President's Cup Final in Dalymount Park, when Shelbourne were leading Shamrock Rovers 1–0 with a minute to play. It was a balmy August evening, and my mind was wandering as I paced the goal. My thoughts had turned to the Crystal Ballroom, where I was going after the game – they were certainly not on the match. I recall looking up into the stand and seeing the trophy being adorned with the red-and-white ribbon, the Shelbourne colours. Suddenly, one of the Rovers players, Tommy Hamilton, took a shot from about forty yards out. It was a very simple shot to save: it must have bounced a dozen times as it came towards me. Somehow, I tripped over my own feet as I was taking the ball and fell into the net with it – to the horror of the Shelbourne players, and indeed myself. Through the net, I saw the shocked face of a man as he whipped the trophy from the stand. The referee blew the final whistle a minute later. We went on to win the replay 3–1.

When I went into work in the brewery the next day, however, I was given a terrible slagging about that goal. The headline on the back page of that morning's *Irish Press* was: 'FLOOD'S FUMBLE FOILS SHELS'. The fourth 'F' came when I read the report! In order to ease my problems, my retort to the slaggers was: 'If you were on £10 to win and £20 to draw, what would you do?'

Unfortunately, this was reported back to the Shelbourne board and, while training the following night, I was called to the boardroom. I had great difficulty explaining that it was only a joke – a defence to the criticism I was getting from every angle.

During the same season, John Heavey, who had come into the club as a reserve goalkeeper, began to put in some tremendous performances. He was preferred as first-team goalkeeper by the manager, Gerry Doyle, during the Shield campaign. Again, fate intervened: just before Shels went to play a friendly match against Morton in Scotland, John was injured, and I was back in the first team. We went to Greenock on a Saturday to play Morton and won 2–1. Paddy Turner, playing inside right, and I had outstanding games; I saved a penalty.

The fact that we had a league match against Bohemians the following day didn't seem to bother the Shels management. We had to fly to Belfast from Glasgow and then travel back to Dublin by coach, eventually arriving home at three in the morning. In those days, Bohemians, whom we had to play on the Sunday, had a mostly amateur team and did not have a high ranking in the league. Even so, they beat us 1–0 that Sunday – a disastrous start to the league for Shelbourne.

A couple of weeks later, following a match in Tolka Park, someone joked that the manager of Morton had been in the stand and had been impressed by some of the team. I paid little attention to this banter and headed home. That night, at a dance in the Garda Headquarters in the Phoenix Park, I was called, from the bandstand, to make my way to the door.

When I went outside, there was a car to take my girlfriend Ann and me to the Gresham Hotel, where I met Hal Stewart, who had recently purchased Morton Football Club. He was interested in signing Paddy Turner, who was also present, and me.

Again, I learned very quickly how to negotiate. As Paddy was a very quiet guy, it was left to me to do all the talking. Hal Stewart offered us full-time contracts to go over to Scotland to play and live there. When I said that I did not want to move out of Dublin, he pointed out to me that I had played in Wales. After I explained how I had travelled over every weekend, he offered to fly both of us over for each match until the end of the season; then, at the end of the season, he would expect us to look seriously at living over there.

The most interesting part of the night was that, when we had completed the discussions and signed the contract, no one had adjusted the terms of the agreement to part-time wages. This meant that we would receive full-time wages. I handed Paddy his contract, folded my own into my pocket and quietly left.

A number of sore points arose when we were transferred. The normal practice was that the club receiving the transfer fee would give something to the player or players being transferred. Shelbourne, however, were adamant that, if Paddy and I looked for anything from them, the deal was off. This obviously presented us with a major problem, as the deal we were getting from Morton – full-time pay for part-time work – was so good that we weren't going to put it in jeopardy.

Another annoyance was Shelbourne's refusal to give me my goalkeeping gear. At that time, most goalkeepers wore yellow jerseys, but I had always worn black. Morton had billed my coming to the club as the arrival of the 'Man in Black'. The black gear was modeled on that of Yashin, the Russian goalkeeper, who was my idol. In the end, I had to buy black gear to bring to Scotland.

Morton was an extremely generous and professional club. At that time Hal Stewart knew very little about football, but he was one of the best motivators of people that I have ever met. I wrote a paper in recent years for the National College of Ireland on leadership skills. I focused on him and Harry Hannon from Guinness as the two people from whom I have learned most about leadership during my life.

Hal was basically an entrepreneur. When we played Celtic in the Scottish Cup, he bought the tenement building adjoining the ground for £3,000 and put advertising, for the cigarettes that his co-op company made, on the side of the wall. He then allocated a platform for the TV cameras directly opposite. For the whole match that Saturday night, the ads were on the screen, as the cameras were unable to avoid them. For his outlay of £3,000, he must have got at least £30,000 worth of advertising!

When, two years later, the club ran into financial difficulties and he had to offload players, he signed eleven free-transfer players – players who had been let go by other clubs. The team made it to the Scottish League Cup Final against Rangers, a match attended by 103,000 people. He was also one of the first people to bring in players from Europe. Long before Continental players came to England, he was bringing them in to Scotland, starting with Sorenson the Danish goalkeeper.

My days in Scotland were idyllic. I finished my mundane job in the brewery on a Friday and, after flying to Scotland, immediately became a star. Over there, Paddy and I were treated very differently from how we'd been treated at Shels. In our first week, Hal Stewart introduced us to everyone at the airport and pointed out that we would be travelling through the airport every weekend and were to be looked after. We stayed in the Queens Park Hotel in Glasgow and travelled down to Greenock for home matches. The people of Greenock treated us as heroes, and the team shot up the league, winning twelve matches after we signed. The fact that they had been signing players right up to our arrival and that everything just seemed to click into place was irrelevant: we got the credit. Paddy and I, because of the media attention we got as a result of flying over every week, were treated like celebrities. My name was unusual in Scotland and was quoted as being the most romantic name in Scottish football!

It was a very strange life – indeed two lives, the high-profile one in Scotland and the drudgery of working in Guinness during the week. We very quickly developed a huge loyalty to the club, and for the first time ever I spent Christmas away from home, playing in the Renfrewshire Cup against St Mirren on Christmas Day. The club left it to ourselves as to whether we would come over for the match or not, as it was the festive season. But despite the trauma of telling our parents that we would be away for Christmas, we felt obliged to travel, as we had been treated so well. It was worthwhile: we won the Remfrewshire Cup 2–1 on the day.

A few days before, on the Saturday before Christmas, we played in Montrose, and I received a bad injury to my eyebrow. On our return to Glasgow, I had to go to hospital to have stitches inserted, but first I had to collect my girlfriend Ann from the airport. She had come over for the weekend, not knowing that I planned to propose to her in Glasgow. After I had been stitched up, we ended up getting engaged in a most romantic setting under the Christmas trees in George's Square – with one of my eyes completely closed!

Unfortunately, the arrangement Paddy and I had made to fly to Glasgow on Saturday morning had to be changed to us flying on the Friday night – when we were snowbound over the new year in Dublin. This period is a key one in Scottish football; we ended up missing two important matches and felt we had let the club down.

During my spell with Morton, we travelled over to play our usual Saturday game in Scotland and then went on by train to London to play Chelsea on Monday night. We stayed on in London and got to watch Rangers and Spurs in White Hart Lane on the Wednesday in the European Cup. This was the era of Dave Mackay, Danny Blanchflower and John White.

We returned to Scotland and during the week trained as full-timers. I experienced the difference between playing part-time and training only three nights a week and having five days free. After practising kick-outs, which I had been doing all morning, my leg locked. I could barely walk and was only just fit for the match on Saturday.

As I have said, the club was exceptionally good to us. Two years later, when they had to cut costs, we offered to play for nothing; unfortunately, they couldn't even afford to bring us back and forth at that stage. Paddy was sold to Celtic and had a great spell with them. I was phoned by Jimmy Scholar, the manager of Bradford, to say that they had agreed my transfer with Morton and to ask when I would be arriving. Morton had not informed me of this, and when I explained that I did not want to live in England, the manager persuaded me to go over for a weekend and that he would try and convince me to stay. By then I was married, and Ann and I went over and were shown around. The men I spoke to reckoned that it was a great club and that I should make the move, but the wives had the opposite view and advised Ann to stay away. The goalkeeper, who wanted to get away from the club, was very positive about me coming over. He obviously wanted to get his replacement in and then move on, and as a result he was unlikely to give the real picture.

Moving to England as a full-timer never really appealed to me. While I loved football, I lacked the courage to make the jump to depending on football to pay the mortgage. Living abroad was also a problem for me: I didn't know whether I'd survive in another country, even one as nearby as England. I have great admiration for those I know who have gone abroad to earn a living, including my son Barry, in New York; my sister Kalleen, thirty-seven years in Paris; and Bernadette, Anne's sister, who went to live in the Middle East.

I subsequently declined the offer from Bradford and ended up with Glentoran in the north of Ireland. My time at Glentoran turned out to be my worst football season ever, from both a playing and a personal point of view. That year, our first child, Sandra, was stillborn. The loss of the child put everything in perspective, and I lost all interest in football. Around that time, I had a disastrous game against Linfield Glentoran, losing 5–1. Halfway through the next season, I was transferred to Sligo. I spent four seasons there before getting a bad injury in the Showgrounds, which ended my football career. As I said to the Glentoran directors during the recent European matches between Glentoran and Shels, Glentoran is the only club I feel I shortchanged in my career.

Playing for Sligo Rovers was certainly an experience. Every second Sunday, nine of us met on O'Connell Bridge. We piled into a minibus and were then driven to Athlone to pick up another player, Jackie Quinn. The only Sligo-based player in the team was David Pugh. The Showgrounds pitch was not the best: at the start of each season, there were hoofprints all over the pitch after the horse show that was held there just before the football season kicked off!

We beat many good teams on that pitch: it was so uneven that it was difficult for good teams to perform well on it! We would adjourn to the Imperial Hotel after home matches for a meal, and most of the guys would spend the night drinking in the bar. I was a teetotaller, so the night tended to drag. I was stone-cold sober when we headed back over the Curlew Mountains late at night in the frost and snow. I was conscious of the crosses on the side of the road, where many others had not made it home. I was amused, reading the *Evening Herald* on Friday nights, when the sports correspondent would speculate that Sligo 'should do well this week', not having to travel.

Sligo Rovers was one of the most honest clubs I had played for, and I had some very happy times there. They honoured every commitment they made and looked after players to the best of their ability. It is still a pleasure for me to travel to their grounds as chairman of Shelbourne. I always receive a warm welcome. We got to the Cup semi-final in 1966, where, sadly, we were beaten by Limerick in a replay. We had scored a perfectly good goal in Tolka Park in the first match, but it was disallowed for offside.

My last game as a professional was against Cork Hibernians in the Showgrounds, playing for Sligo. I was trying to cut out a ball coming in from the wing when I heard an unmerciful crack. My leg had got stuck in a hole which I hadn't seen, as it was full of water. I was carried off on a stretcher, with major damage to my knee. It would have been better if I had broken my leg.

Despite a number of subsequent operations and numerous comebacks, I was unable to play again. So in 1967 my career finished as it had started, against Cork Hibernians. There's more to football than playing in goal, though. My renewed involvement with Shelbourne has proved to be as exciting as those years on the pitch.

*

After I finished playing professional football in 1967, I drifted away from the sport. I had no real involvement at senior football level in the years that followed, although I did get involved in a number of schoolboy teams – Rangers and Dalkey United – in addition to running my own schoolboy team, Ballymun United, when I lived on Ballymun Road. Because I had played as a professional, a number of kids asked me to run a team for them. We had no money, no clubhouse, nothing. All the meetings were held in our small house in Ballymun. We went the whole year without winning a match, until the last game of the year, against Harolds Cross Boys. We were winning 2–1 when the referee blew full-time; it was like winning a cup final. Large bottles of lemonade were produced for everyone; it was magic. Over the years, I watched with satisfaction the progress of the lads in that group.

In the early 1990s, Shelbourne won the league. As managing director of the brewery, I invited the team and officials into James's Gate to celebrate their achievement. Also invited were my teammates from the 1960 Cup-winning side. We had a very pleasant lunch, although Ben Hannigan was not impressed with the young fellows in their blazers 'swanning around without ever having served an apprenticeship'. Ben, when asked at lunch if he had one wish what would it be, modestly replied: 'To sit in the stand in Tolka and watch myself play.'

At the lunch, Ollie Byrne put it to me that the club would like me to become involved at management level. At that stage, Tony Donnelly was the owner and chairman of the club, and Shelbourne was starting out on an ambitious road. Over the years, they had lost their ground at Irishtown, played in Harold's Cross and Dalymount, and generally drifted until they landed in Tolka Park.

The arrival of Tony Donnelly was one of the best things that happened to Shelbourne Football Club. His financial support and enthusiasm enabled Ollie to realise all of his dreams and ideas. Tolka Park was developed, and it became the envy of most League of Ireland clubs. It was a credit to the league and got continuous coverage in the media. In addition, Tony, anxious to win, was very supportive financially in getting in players who were capable of winning the league.

When I went back to the club, it took me a long while to get back into the swing of things and enjoy matches. As I am not a good spectator, I hadn't gone to many matches over the years. Tony, in addition to running his fruit-and-vegetable business in King Street, kept a watchful eye on what was going on at Tolka Park. At the same time, he allowed Ollie a fair degree of latitude.

Tony wanted me to represent the club on public occasions, as he preferred to keep in the background. Being part of the set-up in Tolka gave me a new lease of life, and I took a very active interest in the running of the club. I produced a five-year business plan, something the club had not had before. The management of the club agreed to the implementation of the plan.

While Shelbourne's stadium and facilities were admired by everyone, on the pitch we were erratic. We went through a period where we had Jim McLoughlin and Pat Byrne doing a double act managing the club. This arrangement never seemed to run smoothly for long, as the two of them had very strong personalities. Tony Donnelly, conscious of the friction that might develop between two strong managers, always said that, if one went, they would both have to go. Subsequently, when he decided that Pat Byrne should be sacked, Jim McLoughlin went too. This was very difficult for Tony, because Jim lived near him in Dundalk and was very close to the Donnelly family.

Tony Donnelly, while a successful businessman with his own fruit-and-vegetable business, seemed to enjoy owning a football club and trying to do with the club what he had done with his company. Unfortunately, I don't think Tony fully understood that football clubs are different from businesses in that they usually end up spending money rather than making it!

There is a saying that one way of making a small fortune is to invest a large fortune in a football club. In fact, most of the business people who get involved in the sport, even if they are very successful in their own businesses, are usually hopeless at running the business side of their football club. They usually leave their business brains at home and make poor business decisions, including paying excessive amounts to entice players to come to their clubs.

The Leeds United situation is a very good example of how things can go wrong. In an attempt to buy success, the club spent £90 million on players – money the club did not have. This was all done on the assumption that the team would be one of the top four every year and would thereby qualify to play in European competition. Unfortunately, the results did not go their way, and the club subsequently ran into major financial difficulties and was relegated from the Premiership.

In the 1990s, Shelbourne was very successful. We were in the Cup Final three or four times, we won the league and the Cup, and we played in Europe practically every year. But we also had our difficulties. The dismissal of Pat Byrne and Jim McLaughlin was not handled well, and in hindsight it showed no sensitivity for what they had achieved.

While I was part of the management team at the club, I hadn't really come to the fore or got to the level where I was trusted with tasks such as sacking a manager. Indeed, I think my first management task came in Athens, when there was a disagreement over the bonus to be paid to the players when we played Panathinaikos. Tony asked me to negotiate a deal with the players for the match.

After Pat Byrne and Jim McLoughlin were sacked, Eoin Hand was the manager for a short time before he resigned for personal reasons and headed for South Africa. We then appointed Eamon Gregg as manager. Unfortunately, things did not go well for either Eamon or the club. We were knocked out of the Cup by Limerick in October, and by the time November came, our league season was practically over. I had hung on, hoping that things would improve. They didn't, and banners appeared saying 'SACK THE MANAGER'. Then, when we went to Richmond Park to play St Pats, there was a new banner behind the goal that read: 'SACK THE BOARD AND THE MANAGER'. So the board, in usual football fashion – reacting to pressure from fans – decided to act, and duly relieved Eamon of his duties.

After the departure of Eamon Gregg, we decided to advertise the job in Ireland and England, and we interviewed a number of managers in London and Dublin. We appointed Colin Murphy as manager. He was a member of an inner circle of top managers in England who seem to look after each other. This group includes most of the more prominent and longer-serving Premiership managers.

The Colin Murphy era was quite an experience for Shelbourne in many ways. When he arrived, he was a breath of fresh air: he took a professional approach and would not tolerate any messing from the players. He had various motivational quotes written up in the dressing rooms and was quite philosophical in his utterances.

He was the first manager in all my days in football who did any kind of analysis of the players' wages against the value of their contribution. The first morning I interviewed him in Sutton House in Howth, he produced a matrix to decide whether our most expensive players were indeed our most valuable players. This was quite enlightening: the figures showed that we were not getting value for money in many cases.

Over the years, like most clubs, when we needed a player for a particular position, we often paid over the odds. Market forces dictated, even in football. Colin Murphy's analysis also showed that we were penalising loyalty: players who had been with us for a long time or had come through the schoolboy team were not being paid as well as players who had come in from other clubs.

This seemed unfair to me. One of the first things I did as chairman was to set one scale for senior players and another for younger first-team players. We also had a variety of pay scales for individuals who were learning their trade or trying to gain their place in the team. This enabled us to reassure all the senior professionals in the club that they were all in the same range of salary. It also ensured that those who had shown loyalty to the club were properly rewarded and not taken advantage of.

Colin Murphy left suddenly to run Notts County, and we appointed Damien Richardson to manage the team. Damien managed Shels for three years and was fairly successful but, unfortunately, his era in the club will be remembered mainly for the loss of the league championship in the last match of the season. We had performed well all season and, going into the last match, we needed only a point in Dundalk to guarantee winning the league. St Pats, who were second, had to go to Kilkenny and win, and hope that we lost. As it turned out, on the night we were beaten 1–0 by Dundalk and Pat's won 2–1 in Kilkenny and won the league – much to the joy of Pats manager Pat Dolan. I have never experienced anything like the despair in our dressing room that night: the players were shattered.

During Damien's period as manager, the issue of Wimbledon coming to Dublin arose. The proposal was for Wimbledon FC to relocate to Dublin and play in the Premiership from there. The big spin-off would come if a European league was set up, as Wimbledon would then be the obvious Irish representatives. We, as a club, had taken the view that we were against the Wimbledon project, but Damien went public, singing the praises of the scheme. Although, as a club, we had indicated our opposition to the Wimbledon project, I had met Wimbledon chairman Sam Hamman to discuss the project. Shelbourne believed that Wimbledon coming to Dublin could be quite damaging to the National League, but on the other hand one couldn't ignore the fact that such a move would bring a huge number of tourists into the country: Dublin would have a team capable of attracting thirty thousand people to most home games.

This period was quite traumatic for me: I ended up, quite rightly, being attacked in the media for, on the one hand, holding the line that we were against Wimbledon coming, and at the same time meeting 'Sam the Man'. I can understand people's attitude to me and the club at that time.

Shelbourne was setting standards in football that others had to follow. We became the club that many Irish players wanted to play for. We felt that we had to have the best players: if we heard of a player coming back from England, we tried to sign him. We were, in some people's view, the club that introduced high wages. We started paying players in excess of the market rate, something that put great stress on our finances. So a spiral started that has been difficult to maintain, with problems continuing up to the present day.

We struggled on each year, aided by sponsorship, the money we could bank on for qualifying for Europe, and the support of people who had helped Shelbourne in the past, including Brian Donnelly, Tony's son. In those days, we were spending about £750,000 to keep ourselves going; we are now spending nearly €2 million. The full-time set-up, with all the players and back-room staff working full-time for the club, and the underage section have increased our overheads considerably. The underage section alone costs more than €100,000.

In 1993, Shelbourne went to the Ukraine in the European Cup and had a horrific experience when the plane nearly crashed coming in to land in Lvov. After having descended, the pilot took off again, and the plane went straight up into the darkness. When we landed, we discovered that there had been problems with the undercarriage and the wheels hadn't straightened. We were extremely lucky. That, unfortunately, was Tony Donnelly's last trip: he took ill later in the year and died at Christmas.

The Donnelly family asked me to take over as chairman and help manage the club. I was chuffed with the idea of being chairman of the football club for which I had played. I took a keen interest in what was happening and met with Ollie Byrne two or three times a week at 7 AM to go over all the issues involved in the club. The Donnelly family maintained their interest in the club, with Mrs Donnelly, Brian and Andrew sitting on the board, and Brian taking on his father's role of financing the club and keeping it going. Every so often, Brian would, quite rightly, rattle the cage about the amount of money that was being spent, but, to be fair, I would have to say that, over the years, after an initial outburst he usually picked up the tab and kept the club going.

The football club itself was quite an interesting set-up. The mishmash of characters, personalities and business issues, particularly signing players, were fascinating to me. It was similar to running a small business, with all of the associated problems of finance, marketing and personnel.

During this period, I went to Geneva on a couple of occasions for the European Cup draw. I found the whole operation very interesting. One of the first times I was in Geneva for the draw, Martin Edwards from Manchester United was there; he was rumoured to be trying to sell United for £55 million.

The draw in Geneva attracted numerous TV companies, all in residence in the same hotels as the club delegates. They would invite club representatives to come and talk to them about doing a deal before the draw, in case their club got an Italian, German or French club. They were prepared to pay a fee of $20,000 to $30,000 merely to be given the first option to discuss a deal for televising such games. We learned very quickly that very large sums of money could be made from the TV rights attached to matches and that, if a team drew a French, German or Italian team, the TV rights would be worth a lot more. Over the years, the TV negotiations became more sophisticated; instead of doing negotiations directly with the various TV companies, we employed an agent to negotiate on our behalf.

Over the years, I had some very interesting trips with Shelbourne – to the Ukraine, Iceland, Greece and various other places. Mostly, I enjoyed the ceremony or protocol attached to matches away in Europe: the tradition of players going to the grounds to practise the night before the matches, the club dinner the night before the match – and of course, I also enjoyed it when we won!

During this period of my chairmanship, Bert Millichip, the chairman of the English FA, was the UEFA representative at Tolka Park during one of our matches. We were led to believe that he could be difficult in terms of his expectations, so I was delegated by Ollie to look after him. I took him for a spin out to Dalkey and Dun Laoghaire, and we spent a long part of the afternoon in the Silver Tassie in Loughlinstown, where he opened up. Among other things, we discussed the difficulties facing the chairman of Marseilles, Bernard Tapie, who was a possible presidential candidate in France at the time.

When we played Panathinaikos in Athens, we attended the pre-match dinner the night before the game. We were having our drinks when one of the directors of Panathinaikos informed us that the owner of the club, who was a multi-millionaire, was about to board his helicopter on his yacht in the bay. We were told that he would land in four minutes and be in the room in six minutes. This he duly did, to the second, arriving in exactly six minutes later. I remember sitting with him at dinner that night and being fascinated by his continued use of the worry beads which he carried with him. I think Ollie was tempted to offer him the chance to buy into Shelbourne – in which case Ollie presumably would have expected to have his own heli-copter!

Usually, at the draw in Geneva we would meet with clubs we were drawn against, to make the arrangements for travelling to their country. One particular year, we drew Akranes, an Icelandic team. Their representative told us that the players would find it tiring driving to the ground from Reykjavik, and therefore we should stay in Akranes and that he would make the accommodation arrangements. We subsequently found ourselves staying in what was basically a hostel – for which we were paying. The town was practically closed down from 8 PM, and there was nothing for our supporters. It was one of the most unsatisfactory trips that we had in all of our travels.

On another occasion, when we landed in the Ukraine to play Karpathia, we were met by a guy in a white suit and a black shirt, who informed us that our hotels had been changed and that we would be going to different hotels. Ollie Byrne, who had had a similar experience a couple of years earlier in the Ukraine, when the club was forced to move to a Mafia-owned hotel, refused point-blank to be moved again. At 2 AM, he was dancing up and down in front of our interpreter, a middle-aged woman, shouting at her: 'Tell him we may be f—ing Irish but we're not f—ing green!' The translator was looking blankly at me and trying to decipher what he was saying. I couldn't help her, though, because I couldn't stop laughing watching the pantomime in front of me: the guy in the white suit and black shirt refusing to budge, Ollie jumping up and down, swearing, and the rest of us standing around wondering where we were going to put our heads down for the night. It was quite a scene! In the end, Ollie won out and we ended up in the hotel we had booked originally.

Two years before, the players had had stomach upsets as a result of the food in the Ukraine. After that, Joe Corcoran, who looked after the international team, oversaw all the cooking. Although we had brought all our food with us on that trip, we needn't have worried, as we were in a first-class hotel and the food was excellent. As well as the hold full of food, I had brought crates of canned draught Guinness, half of which was to go on to Georgia with the Linfield team, who were sharing our plane. All the beer was to have been kept in the hold of the plane and not consumed until after the matches. When we had the near-accident, the Linfield players, who were going to have to hang around for two or three more hours, demanded that the Guinness be taken out of the hold and opened. It certainly helped to settle everyone's nerves! We brought the rest of Guinness into the Ukraine and opened it after the match. We ended up distributing it outside the hotel to the flower ladies and others. There was a great party on the footpath outside the hotel.

A few weeks later, when Karpathia FC, from Lvov in the Ukraine, landed at Dublin Airport for the return match, they claimed they had no money for landing charges or fuel. A heated debate ensued, with them claiming they had no money and Ollie Byrne and I, who had travelled to the airport to meet them, saying that there was nothing we could do about it. Ollie had experienced problems in travelling in Europe before and was up to most of the dodges that were likely to be encountered. After initially saying that they would all sleep on the plane and only come off for the match, they suddenly produced a briefcase full of American dollars and emptied it out onto the table to pay whatever fees or dues they were supposed to pay!

For the return match in Dublin, the Ukrainians brought a number of businessmen with them, including a brewer from Llov. We had a reception in Guinness for them the night before the match, and I showed the brewer around our brewery. Halfway through the tour, he said he had seen enough – apparently he was quite depressed, given the high-tech state of our brewery compared to the one he worked in. I heard later that his brewery had done a deal with Coca-Cola, though, so presumably things improved for him.

In 1995, we had our centenary: on three consecutive nights we had Leeds United, Manchester United and Liverpool in Tolka Park. This was a tremendous achievement and a great credit to Ollie Byrne, who managed to get the agreement of the three teams to play in Dublin. Indeed, Sky Sports was so surprised to discover that one club was able to attract the 'big three' clubs from England that they did a half-hour feature on the three matches. This was probably a tremendous boost for tourism too, because they also filmed in Glendalough and other areas outside Dublin. They were three great days, with all the hustle of the organisation, the logistics, the general pressure of allocating tickets, and everything else that goes into organising a festival of football.

In true Shelbourne fashion, thinking big, in 1994, the year of the World Cup in the USA, we decided that we would hire the big screen that had been used at the Winter Olympics at Lillehammer, Norway, to show the Ireland games against Italy, Norway and Mexico on the big screen in Tolka. We were hoping that, as it was June, the beautiful weather would attract families to come to Tolka, where there would be a picnic atmosphere. There was also to be a major bingo game on the Sunday after the Italy match, featuring huge prizes and compèred by Pat Kenny. People would travel from all over Ireland to Tolka for the bingo event – or so we hoped.

Although there was a lot of prize money for the bingo, we had calculated we would make a significant amount of money. In fact, we lost more than £100,000 on the deal because, after Ireland beat Italy on the Saturday, the euphoria carried over to Sunday. People were still celebrating, or suffering from hangovers, and really didn't want to travel for bingo. We were committed to the prize money, however, and had to go ahead, despite the poor attendance.

In 1995, Brian Donnelly decided to get out of football for business reasons. He suggested that I take over the club with a clean balance sheet: he was prepared to pay all its debts. After weeks of discussion between our two legal representatives, Brian changed his mind and decided to stay on at the club. I was just as happy to see him stay but would have preferred not to have incurred the legal costs that were involved in what turned out to be a wasted exercise.

By 1996, Brian Donnelly decided that Damien Richardson was not achieving the necessary success for the club and that he should be relieved of his duties. The resulting negotiations in relation to his departure led me to walk away from Shelbourne Football Club. I decided to resign as chairman and leave the football scene altogether.

If I had thought my leaving would have a major effect on the club, I was left in no doubt that it was of little consequence when only two people bothered to indicate to me that they were sorry I was going: Ollie Byrne's sister Carmel and his brother Andy, who wrote me a nice letter. Subsequently, two or three people did mention to me that they were sorry I had resigned. Cormac Farrell, another director, resigned with me. The episode reminded me, if I needed reminding, how fickle sports people can be.

In the ensuing period under Gary Browne's chairmanship, Shelbourne had a tremendous spell, in which they won the league and Cup double. Shels also played Rangers in Scotland and in the European Cup; in fact, they were winning 3–0 against Rangers before going on to lose 5–3 – a great performance. While I was out of football, I took an interest in the fortunes of Shels from afar but didn't really regret not being involved. Apart from anything else, it gave me more time to spend with my grandson Josh.

In 2000, the Donnelly family decided that they wanted to get out of Shelbourne, and Gary Browne also decided to step down, for personal reasons. There was a feeling that, if the Donnellys pulled out and Gary left, Shelbourne would be seen to be in some kind of trouble. Ollie and Colm Murphy approached me to ask if I would come back as chairman. Initially, I was completely against it and would not even consider it, given the circumstances in which I had left. When Ollie said that 'It is in the interest of the club', I decided I would go back as chairman – albeit that it was my clearly stated position that I would not be involved in the day-to-day running of the club but would merely act as a figurehead. Everybody agreed to this – but, of course, they subsequently expected me to fulfil exactly the same duties as I had done the first time, something I have steadfastly refused to do.

When I went back, the club had gone full-time professional and it was clear to me that this state of affairs was putting major financial strain on the club. We were really investing in the players in the hope that we would get through the early rounds of the European Competition and then into the Champions League group stages, in which case we could make a lot of money. During my absence, the club had had discussions with Rosenborg of Norway and Bronby of Denmark and other clubs about the amount of money that could be made from qualification for the play-off stages in Europe. We were told by Rosenborg that they had made £19 million from it. Our view was that, with some help from a financial backer, we would have a reasonable chance of making the breakthrough in Europe.

A huge disappointment awaited us when, having drawn Hibernians of Malta in 2002 – a relatively easy draw – and having gone there and drawn 2–2, we were beaten 1–0 in the return leg at Tolka Park, going down to a goal scored in the ninety-first minute. This was a major blow for the club, both financially and emotionally, and set us back by about five years.

Because Shelbourne are playing in seven different locations around the city and because of the lack of space for us to expand in Tolka Park, we decided to move to a new stadium. With that in mind, we have looked to have Tolka Park rezoned as suitable for residential development, on the understanding that all of the money accumulated from the sale, after debts are paid, will go towards funding the new stadium. This money will be put in trust so that it cannot be used by us or our successors for any other purposes.

The move out of Tolka Park will be an emotional one, given the history of the ground and all the great names and teams that have played there over the years. At the moment, however, finance is a big problem for all football clubs: when one looks at the number of teams that have got into financial difficulties and ended up in administration in England, it is clear that the way ahead will continue to be very difficult for Shelbourne. However, with good planning and management – and a little luck – we will continue to make progress.

Unless there is a major breakthrough in European competitions by an Eircom League side within the next five years, there is no way that full-time football can be justified or maintained by any League of Ireland team. The gates this year, despite the shift from winter to summer soccer, are down. Summer soccer does not seem to be the attraction that everyone thought it would be, although it has greatly helped the teams playing in Europe by giving them a better chance when they are playing teams that are already well into their seasons.

In the past, winning the league or the Cup was the key objective of clubs, but for those who are making big investments in full-time football, the objective has now switched to progressing to the group stage of the Champions – which could bring in up to €6 million from UEFA's central marketing fund, not to mention the sums that would be generated from gate receipts.

Shelbourne believe that it is a very realistic ambition for an Irish club to qualify for the group stages of the Champions League in the next five years, provided that there is a robust business plan to finance the increased cost. We believe that Shelbourne, of all the clubs in the league, is the one best positioned to achieve this breakthrough.

Having expectations of competing in the Champions League Group Stages successfully is not as far-fetched as it might seem, as clubs like Rosenborg and Bromby have already made the leap – and benefited from the resulting financial bonanza. Shelbourne has played both of these clubs in European competition in recent years and, during our visits to these clubs, having listened to them explain the financial benefits of their success, we are convinced that it is possible for an Irish club to do the same. It should be pointed out, however, that in the cases of both of these clubs, significant new investors – from both the state and the private sector – emerged to help fund their European breakthrough.

In line with the strategy of the successful clubs in small countries like our own, Shelbourne has developed a thriving underage football section comprising seventeen teams. These include some of the best young soccer talent in the country. An emphasis on youth football seems to us to be a prerequisite for success in Europe, and Shelbourne has moved to put that important foundation stone in place. The future is about European football, and possibly a European league, with domestic leagues only a means of getting there.

*

When I went back to Shelbourne, I was asked to sit on the FAI executive, representing the club. I accepted the offer and did the job for a number of years, during which time I was elected to various committees, including the finance committee. At that time, the officers were all powerful people – Joe Delaney, Michael Hyland, Des Casey, Pat Quigley and Louis Kilcoyne. I found a lot of the working arrangements different from what I was familiar with, and there seemed to be an abdication of power by the executive to the officer board. The officers appeared to rule supreme, and signs of opposition or questioning of the running of the Association were not encouraged.

Many of the members on the executive were genuinely interested in the future of football, but quite a number were conscious of the fact that they could be easily removed by those who had put them in their position. My experience was that it was not unusual for people who were creating problems within the executive of the FAI to find themselves under pressure back at their clubs: their behaviour at council could affect the FAI's attitude to the particular club or organisation they represented. This practice was never obvious but became apparent to me over the years. Nonetheless, I enjoyed my early days in the FAI. The work was interesting and gave me a good insight into the running of the organisation.

I travelled to America with the international team in 1994 as part of the official FAI party. We attended the win in New York against Italy, the draw in Orlando against Mexico, and the draw in New York again against Norway. The trip was dominated by debate on the heat, and particularly Jack Charlton's obsession about the team being denied access to water during the matches. The arguments over whether extra water supplied should be allowed on the pitch dominated the discussions before the Norway match – to the extent that some commentators began to question whether the debate might affect the players more than the problem itself. Jack Charlton had been banned from the sideline for this match and watched the play from a TV gantry.

In many areas, the FAI was very efficient, particularly in terms of its contacts with UEFA and its involvement on the international scene at representative level. Maybe this was because there were lots of benefits for individuals from making these connections – acting as observers at matches or sitting on committees. One of the other perks of such work was regular trips abroad.

During the course of my time on the executive, Jack Charlton stood down after the play-off match in Liverpool with Holland, when we were beaten 2–0. The pressure appeared to be on from some people in the officer brigade to have Charlton removed. It was rumoured that he had in fact agreed to step down after that match but had later changed his mind. One way or another, the manager's job became vacant.

I suppose it is an indication of how the Association was run that, while I was a member of the executive and the finance committee, I didn't really know the background to the Charlton resignation or dismissal. I wasn't kept up to date or briefed, and neither, to my knowledge, were most of the other members of the executive.

My views in relation to the recruitment of a new manager were that a new manager should have overall responsibility for football both in Ireland and for our players competing at international level overseas. Most of all, he should be responsible for – or at least be involved in – the development of the game at all levels. Jack Charlton had done a wonderful job of putting Ireland on the football map, but in terms of leaving a legacy of young players or setting up structures for the future, he and his assistant Maurice Setters had done relatively little.

When the subject of the appointment of an international manager came up for discussion, I asked what the job specification was, and whether the job would be advertised. Some of the officers were particularly hostile to the idea of a job specification being drawn up, arguing that you couldn't have a job specification for people of the calibre that we would be considering for the manager's job. The view was also expressed that 'people like this' would not come for interview and that we should head-hunt them instead. This made me very uneasy – and suspicious, perhaps unfairly, that the decision on who would be appointed might already have been made.

It was agreed at the October–November 1995 executive meeting that the officers should come up with proposals for a job specification and draft plans for the international manager, and that these would then be put to the executive at the January meeting. When we came to the January meeting, however, the job specification and draft plan had not been produced. Fortunately, I had produced my own draft plan, which I presented to the council.

This draft specification was debated and was subsequently

accepted by the council as the framework whereby a new manager would be selected. Major emphasis was placed on the development of youth policies and on the creation of an infrastructure to support the development of young players, who would be brought on to the international team. It was clear that the new management team would have a completely different brief from the one that had existed in the Jack Charlton era and would be responsible for both ensuring the supply of players to the international team and helping to improve the national league. Although the manager did not have to be personally involved in all these areas of activity, he had to take overall responsibility for the future of football in the country on a technical level.

The executive, having accepted my draft proposal, decided that the interview panel for the manager's job would consist of the five officers, with the addition of myself, as I had drawn up the job specification. I'm not sure that this sat too well with the officers, but they had no choice in the matter. As it turned out, Des Casey was unable to attend any of the interviews, and the task of selecting a new manager was left to four officers and myself.

The interviews were to be held in England over a number of days at a secret location. To my surprise, the media were already there when we arrived at the hotel; in fact, Louis Kilcoyne was giving an interview to Sky Sports. Louis felt that, as the TV company had found the hotel, he, as president of the FAI, should talk to them.

After the initial interviews, it was decided to short-list and have a second day of interviews. At this stage, Joe Kinnear, a strong candidate for the job, decided to withdraw his application, stating that, while he was very interested in the job itself, the timing was wrong for him, and maybe next time around would be better for him. During this time, I became aware that most people involved in football had a favoured journalist – as I suppose I also had – whom they supplied with information.

Following the final interviews, a debate took place on the merits of each candidate. While panel members obviously had their preferences, we all also had very strong objections to particular candidates. In some cases, members were nearly as strong in their opposition to certain people getting the job as they were in support of others. At the end of the day, we failed to reach agreement on a candidate and flew back to Dublin. On the plane home, Pat Quigley and I decided that we should try to get the selection completed that night. We decided to get a hotel room in Dublin Airport and stick with it until we had made a selection. Nothing new was going to be added to our information at that stage.

We discussed the position at the Airport Hotel: it it is no secret that eventually, by majority vote, Mick McCarthy, then manager of Milwall, was selected for the job. Again, some of the panel, anxious that we wouldn't go backwards, insisted that Mick be phoned and offered the job there and then. At 11.30 that night, Louis Kilcoyne phoned Mick, who was not enamoured to be rung at that hour, particularly as Louis was, as had been agreed by the interview panel, trying to get him to make a decision on the spot.

Mick eventually took the job – but then headed into the most unmerciful turmoil in the history of the FAI. He had been appointed only a few days when, in a radio interview, Louis made it clear that Mick was not his choice and that he would not have picked him as manager of the international team. From a PR point of view, this was a disaster: it undermined Mick considerably. In addition, Mick encountered problems when he tried to appoint Ian Evans, who had been with him at Milwall, as his number two. The FAI would not agree to his appointment and added further to the problems by indicating that they wanted to dismiss some of the staff who were already involved with the international team. Mick was reluctant to let these people go.

I was travelling to Galway when I heard what Louis had said about the selection of Mick McCarthy. I was furious, particularly as I had been involved in the selection and knew how things had gone. I rang Sean Connolly, CEO of the FAI, who spoke to Joe Delaney; Joe agreed that Louis's comments were most inappropriate and that the FAI should issue a statement fully backing Mick. Sean was charged with organising this. That night at dinner in Galway, however, I received a message to ring Sean, who told me that Louis had decided that no statement on the issue would be made. The whole matter turned into a big row at the FAI executive when I, in criticising the fact that a statement had not gone out, asked Louis directly why this was the case. He said that he had had advice not to put it out. Clearly, in my mind, there was an agreement that a statement would go out, and this agreement had been changed. The row paled into insignificance, however, when, a short time later, it was reported that there had been some problem with ticket sales for the Republic of Ireland's matches in Sweden in 1988! It was initially alleged that money had been lost by the FAI to a dealer who had sold black-market tickets. Veronica Guerin was investigating the story.

Around the same time, and completely unrelated, problems arose for Sean Connolly. It became clear that he would have to leave the FAI, and he duly resigned. In the following Saturday's papers, an article appeared claiming that two of the officers were going to share the post between them and go full-time on the administration side. Again, I got myself involved – I don't know why! – and rang Joe Delaney. I told Joe that this was most inappropriate; in my view, it was not good for the Association. Joe Delaney and I met in the Tara Hotel that Saturday afternoon and discussed the situation. He agreed that this approach was not appropriate and that it would not happen.

At that meeting, Joe asked me what exactly I wanted in the Association – a subject to which, quite frankly, I had never previously given any thought. I had found myself caught up in the activities of the FAI and probably became more involved than I should have. Looking back on it, I think it was a period of madness on my part: I allowed myself to become involved in many issues about which the majority of people in football in Ireland did not really care.

Joe asked me if I was interested in one of the officer posts. I said that I would be but that I wasn't interested in getting one by some skulduggery. I said to him that, if such a post was offered to me, I would certainly take it, because at that time I had a keen interest in the whole running of the Association. On top of Sean Connolly's departure, however, the problem in relation to ticket money had escalated.

The officers held a press conference and denied that an officer of the FAI had put money into the Association to cover up any loss, as had been reported, and that at no time had the FAI been short of money for tickets. Two days later, the officers had to go back to the press and admit that there had been a problem with ticket money and that one of the officers had put a significant amount of money into the pot to cover up the loss of money due to the non-payment for tickets by a ticket tout.

This unleashed a huge scandal, but at the press conference on the Wednesday that first dealt with the money issue, a reporter raised the lack of support for Mick McCarthy and his appointment, and the fact that I had indicated that a supportive statement was to have been issued and had not been. Some of the officers denied that it had ever been agreed that a statement would be issued. One reporter, who subsequently contacted me, said that he had asked the officers sitting at the top table if they were calling me a liar, and they repeated that there had never been any agreement to issue a statement.

When I heard this, I decided that I'd had enough and resigned from the Association. I decided that I didn't want to work with people who operated in this fashion. Some officers, I am sure, were delighted to see the end of me. Evelyn Owens, the then chairman of the Labour Court, asked me the day I resigned: 'Do you really want all that s– in your life?'

At this stage, however, the issue of the ticket money had snowballed. The media had suddenly woken up to the fact that all was not well in Merrion Square – an amazing fact, given the closeness of the media not just to Merrion Square but to individuals within it. Suddenly, the media, who had previously benefited from their close links to people in the FAI, were now calling for blood and lambasting the FAI.

I met Des Casey on the Friday, when the news had broken that there was a problem and that money had in fact been put in by an officer of the Association. I asked him what his position was, and he replied that he was going to Malta with one of the youth teams and that he would think about it for the week and then decide what to do. After careful consideration, he decided, in the wider interest of football, to stay on.

A call was made in the media for all the officers to resign. The pressure built up, and eventually four of the officers resigned and decided to seek a vote of confidence from the executive the following Friday. Louis Kilcoyne resisted calls for him to resign and stayed in office. By the end of the Friday meeting, which went on well into the night, Joe Delaney resigned, and Louis Kilcoyne was out of office. Des Casey, Michael Hyland and Pat Quigley were reappointed.

I felt very sorry for Joe and his family, as I knew the effect that this would have on them. Joe was a most able administrator and worked extremely hard to modernise the Association. Unfortunately, although I was out of the FAI at this stage, because of what had happened to Joe and presumably due to his perception of Shelbourne, at this time I lost the friendship of someone with whom I had enjoyed a close relationship over my years in football. It must have given Joe great satisfaction to see the rise of his son John to the top post in the FAI.

This was one of the most dramatic periods in the Association – one of complete turmoil and acrimony. One problem seemed to follow another, and although most of these problems were not connected, they all ended up being rolled in together.

Subsequently I have had no involvement in the FAI. However, having been approached and asked to apply for the CEO post after Brendan Menton left, I did apply but, on 'mature reflection' then withdrew my application.

\*

In the fifties and sixties, the League of Ireland, as it was then known, managed to attract huge crowds to Milltown and Tolka Park most weeks, with the grounds full to overflowing when local derbies were taking place. During that period, a number of families dominated the soccer scene, with the Proles running Drumcondra in Tolka Park, the Cunninghams running Rovers in Milltown, and Shelbourne, which was run by Danny Traynor and Gerry Doyle, playing out of Tolka and Dalymount as tenants.

For those two decades, the League of Ireland formed a major part of the social fabric of life, particularly in Dublin. Sport and dancing were the entertainment of the weekends, the dance-hall era being at its height. Even the pubs were not as big an attraction – or maybe this was just my imagination. With competition from television and cheap travel to Britain to watch the Premiership clubs increasing, the league has struggled, and crowds have diminished. Today, hundreds of people leave the country to go to Old Trafford, Anfield or Elland Road for matches, both at the weekend and mid-week, and all around the country young children wear the jerseys of the various Premiership clubs and idolise Premiership players.

While people are travelling to England to see the big teams play there, the market for the same teams playing friendlies here has changed dramatically in recent years. The only time we at Shelbourne can be sure of success in bringing over a Premiership club is when we bring in Manchester United. While Liverpool would probably make money for us now, having won the Champions League, the old days, when Leeds United regularly came to play us and we made money from their appearances, are gone. In recent years, our friendly match with Celtic has lost more than €100,000. As there is so much football on television, bringing over the British clubs is no guarantee of a full stadium.

The League of Ireland – now the Eircom League – has suffered badly as a result of these social changes, and the success of the international team has put further pressure on the league. While the FAI will rightly argue that the success of the international team has funded major developments in soccer in Ireland, funding many league clubs through grants that are then used to develop grounds, overall it has had an adverse effect on the Eircom League. It seems that, the more successful the international team, the less the interest in the national league.

The Eircom League is struggling, with clubs at one end of the spectrum operating on a shoestring, and at the other end clubs spending significant amounts of money they they do not have in order to be successful. This is a vicious circle: once you are on the treadmill of success, you can't afford to get off it. The consequences are that more and more football clubs continually operate on a knife edge. Moreover, any examination of the structure of the league clubs over the last ten to fifteen years will show that, despite business people coming into the game to finance clubs for short periods of time, most of them drift away within three or four years.

In the Eircom League, many clubs haven't really made up their minds what they want to be. Do they want to be part of the big boys' club, investing lots of money, having lots of success, and accumulating lots of debts, or do they want to run clubs where spending is strictly controlled and they have very little to worry about on the financial side – and, equally, very little success? This is a dilemma not only for the clubs but for the league and the FAI in the next few years.

In any business environment, the product is the key to success. The quality of the product, together with the presentation, delivery and price of the product, all play a part in whether the enterprise is a success or not. Unfortunately, the Eircom League has never marketed its product with sufficient backing or funds to enable it to progress. The introduction in 2005 of the Setanta Cup, involving the top clubs in the North and South, was a great step forward.

For soccer in Ireland to compete with Gaelic games, rugby and the English Premiership requires sustained support from the FAI or the Eircom League. Every so often, these organisations invest money in the sport and claim that they have got coverage, or commitment to coverage, from TV stations, but the reality is that the financial support necessary to get the product off the ground has not been available until now. John Delaney has managed to get significant financial backing for football in Ireland in his short time in office.

Shelbourne's involvement in European competition in 2004, particularly the game against Deportivo La Coruña in Lansdowne Road, did more for the league than all previous efforts had. People were surprised at the quality of the football that Shelbourne played, and even those who did not follow football were all of a sudden taking an interest in it. We could have sold another ten thousand tickets for the match at Lansdowne.

The current situation in the Eircom League is that a rift has grown between the smaller, low-budget clubs and the bigger clubs, who are run more like businesses and have developed their teams to compete in Europe. The target for most Eircom League clubs is to qualify for Europe and hope to get a bonanza draw and make significant money. While this may be the objective, I have to say I have reservations as to whether it is realistic to expect that a financial bonanza will result merely from qualifying for Europe. Certainly, sizeable prize money is available for qualifying for the UEFA Cup, but when one takes into account the travelling expenses attached to competing in the first and second rounds, and players' bonuses, very often any profit made by the club is minimal.

There have been exceptions, particularly when clubs are drawn against a major club with attractive television coverage in Italy, France or Germany. Bohemians, for instance, made significant money when they drew Bordeaux some years ago.

The Eircom League is currently at a crossroads. There are teams vying with the top teams in Europe to qualify for the Champions League group play-offs. There are others paying out money they cannot afford in order just to run on the spot, and there are others who are really only 'playing with the train set'. Which of these groups it is better to be part of is debatable, as each of them have their merits. Last season, when I was talking to Doug Ellis, chairman and owner of Aston Villa, he argued very forcefully that his club was one of the few in England that was in the black and that he was extremely proud of this fact. While Villa hadn't won trophies recently, they were still in the Premiership and benefiting from significant TV money.

There is a lot to be said for running a club and keeping it in the black, particularly when all around, clubs are getting into serious financial problems. In England in the last few years, a significant number of clubs have gone into administration. Without success, however, a club will fade and die. The lifeblood of football is success: whether winning trophies, playing in Europe, or getting the club a profile across the football world.

It doesn't help the Eircom League that there is no set day of the week for the matches to be played. In the old days of playing on Sunday, everyone knew when the matches were on, so soccer became part of people's routine. Nowadays, it can vary between Friday night, Saturday night and Sunday, due mainly to the timing of European Cup matches. Unless somebody decides exactly where the Eircom League is going and plans a strategy accordingly, football in Ireland will go downhill rapidly over the next few years.

One solution would be for clubs to share stadia in order to save money: this option has to be considered for the future. For that reason, we at Shelbourne are in discussions with Bohemian Football Club with a view to sharing Dalymount Park. Coming to an agreement will require considerable goodwill from both the two clubs and the FAI.

Many critics argue that there is no sense in trying to do anything with the Eircom League as it has no chance of going anywhere. It's worth remembering that, a few years ago, hurling in this country appeared to be doomed. Over the last five years, there has been a tremendous resurgence in the sport. The sport, which has been highly successful in attracting spectators, is at last being seen as the skilled game that it is. Significant credit for the turnaround should go to the sponsors, my old employers, Guinness. Hurling now enjoys massive media coverage – an area where the Eircom League has, over the years, fallen down. This, we hope, is about to change, with a commitment to more extensive TV coverage across RTÉ, TV3 and Setanta.

The media have over the years paid little attention to the Eircom League, except in a crisis. The daily newspapers cover the Eircom League on particular days of the week, but I know from talking to reporters that they have great difficulty in getting support from their editors to cover issues relating to the Eircom League. Indeed, the editor of one of the major daily papers said to me some years ago that he would put a report on a junior cricket match from Pakistan into his paper rather than cover the Eircom League. The only time the league gets major coverage is if there is a row going on between clubs, a breakdown between the Eircom League and the FAI, or some other type of in-fighting.

The ongoing bickering and bad publicity surrounding soccer in Ireland – both within the FAI and between clubs – also does nothing to encourage sponsorship. Neither do the threats of legal action help the image of the game. If all the money that has been spent over the years on legal battles had been pooled, it would have greatly helped the finances of the league.

Given that qualification for Europe by winning the league leaves a club only three matches away from the Champions League group stages, it is extraordinary that nobody has decided to buy a national league club and invest money to turn it into another Rosenborg. (Rosenborg made something like £19 million out of qualifiying for the play-offs in Europe.) This is an opportunity awaiting a club in Ireland that has the financial resources and the playing staff to do what Rosenborg did. At the moment, however, the clubs trying to achieve this breakthrough are doing it on a shoestring, with exorbitant wage bills and without the necessary financial backing.

The running of the expensive clubs we played in Europe in 2004 highlighted the cost of competing in Europe: Deportivo La Coruña spent €80 million per annum and Lille €32 million – quite a contrast to our €2 million. The returns for success are massive, however: Lille, for instance, made €17 million in one season's campaign.

The league clubs are also going to have to tackle their expenditure, particularly the huge amounts of money spent on players' salaries. Very often, clubs struggle to ensure that the players get their salaries; then, when an opportunity arises for the club to get an influx of cash through a good draw in the Champions League or a match with a Premiership team, some players immediately stick their hands out and look for more. They seem to forget that, as with any business, the income accumulated over the season from various functions is necessary to keep them in employment.

The wheel has turned full circle from the draconian contracts of the 1950s to the present situation, when players earn ridiculously high wages. Indeed, the sight of Premiership players kissing the club badge or the jersey is, in many cases, a bad joke, given that in some instances the same players are already looking to move to another club.

In the past, a player tended to be known as a Shels, Rovers, Cork player, and stayed with the one club for their whole careers. Players, with a few exceptions, now move at the drop of a hat and have little loyalty to any club. While the players will argue that, over the years, they have struggled, and that on occasions clubs haven't paid them their wages, the more reputable clubs have honoured their contracts in the most difficult of circumstances.

My own club, Shelbourne, was probably instrumental in creating an artificial level of income in the Eircom League, which has resulted in very ordinary players being paid money to play football, mediocre players being paid even more money, and good players getting significant salaries. The current levels of expenditure cannot be justified based on the incomes enjoyed by clubs.

Currently, the only time we get a big gate is in the local Dublin derbies against Rovers, Pats or Bohs. Very little extra comes when there are visitors from outside the Pale. Having teams located all over the country is obviously in the interest of football overall, but from a business perspective it is of no benefit whatever to clubs like us. The more derby matches, within reason, the more money can be made at the gates. One of the sad ironies of the sport is that the interests of football, as a whole, are sometimes in conflict with a club's requirements for finance.

*

In the mid-1990s, when Shelbourne set out to make a breakthrough in European football, most people thought that this was not achievable and was just a dream. As I write this in my hotel in La Coruña in Spain in 2004, I realise that even the most optimistic of us over the years probably had doubts that we could make the dream a reality, particularly after our elimination from the Champions League, by Hibernians of Malta, two years ago.

Winning the Eircom League in 2003 guaranteed our entry into European competition. This started with a trip to Reykjavik, to play AK Reykjavik, which looked like it was destined for disaster when the home team went two-up against us. Although the score remained 2–0 with about ten minutes to go, two late goals, one by Alan Moore and another an own goal, changed the complexion of the return game in Tolka Park.

Despite the tension, and the awareness of the consequences of failure, the team performed on the night in Dublin and duly eliminated AK Reykjavik in the first round, which brought us on to Hajduk Split in Croatia. We knew Hajduk Split would be at least a step up from the teams we had played in the first round. Despite the fact that they had a tremendous reputation, we came away with a 2–1 defeat – and, most importantly, an away goal.

Even before they came to Dublin, Hajduk Split had accused our players of being over-physical. On the night of the match, their technical football coach complained to the referee about the ground, the markings – and virtually everything else about Tolka Park. He made a big mistake, however, when he went on TV3 the night before the match and publicly stated that defeat for them would spell financial ruin. This was a staggering statement to make publicly twenty four hours before the match and demonstrated the pressure under which Hajduk Split were playing.

Tolka Park had one of its biggest crowds for many years, and we played some of the best football that I have seen over the years from a Shelbourne team. In the first half, the players were magnificent and should have gone two or three goals up. The Hajduk Split goalkeeper made a number of spectacular saves, one of them being similar to the famous save by Gordon Banks in the World Cup in South America against Brazil.

In the second half, Shels continued to dominate, but it was only ten minutes from the end that the magic goal – a likely contender for goal of the season – came from Dave Rogers. Tolka Park went mad! This wasn't the end of it, though, and in the last few minutes Shels got a second goal, to clinch the tie.

To say that Hajduk Split's directors and supporters were shocked was an understatement. The directors afterwards were speechless: I could see that there were going to be major consequences for them. In fact, three days later we heard that they had announced they might have to go into administration.

For us, it was a night to savour. It reminded me of a night nearly twelve years before when we had knocked the Ukrainian team Karpathia out of the European Cup 2–1 – the night of Brian Mooney's never-to-be-forgotten goal from thirty yards out.

On that occasion, the Ukrainians had agreed with us when we were in the Ukraine that any television money arising from the second leg of that tournament, from the match with Panathinaikos of Greece, would be shared between our two clubs, regardless of which of us got through. Having beaten us 1–0 at home, however, when they arrived in Dublin they announced that they weren't prepared to honour the agreement and that it was winner-take-all. In the circumstances, winning through gave us great satisfaction.

When we beat Hajduk Split, we knew that we were going out

to meet Deportivo La Coruña, who were beaten Champions League semi-finalists in 2003 and one of the leading clubs in Europe: the draw had been made before the return game in Dublin. The attraction of meeting one of the top teams in Europe was something that we had savoured for days leading up to the match with Hajduk Split, hoping that we could get through.

On the night we beat Hajduk Split, a representative of Deportivo La Coruña was in the crowd, and we immediately entered into discussions with him to try to have the fixture against Deportivo reversed, so that the first leg was played in Dublin. We had been drawn away in the first leg. They very graciously agreed to switch, and we spent the next twenty-four hours getting agreement to the change from UEFA. Faxes passed backwards and forwards clarifying what we proposed to do.

Within minutes of the game finishing in Tolka, we had discussions with FAI CEO Fran Rooney, with a view to getting Lansdowne Road for the match, if we needed it. There was a lot of debate and controversy in Shelbourne as to whether we should shift the game, with the manager, Pat Fenlon, emphatically stating that he wanted to play the tie in Tolka Park. Having had discussions with Pat and Ollie Byrne, I decided as chairman that I should make the decision. This was agreed, so that, if there was to be any accusation made in relation to the transfer, I would be responsible for justifying the decision.

Within the next twelve hours, and early on the Thursday morning following our win, the whole nation seemed to be alive with the excitement of what we had achieved. This was the first time an Irish team had made it into the third round of the competition. We were only ninety minutes away from playing in the group stages of the Champions League. Bring on Manchester United, Real Madrid or anyone else!

It was clear that we could not handle the fixture in Tolka Park, not just because of the number of people who would want to see the match against the Spaniards, but also because of the administrative difficulties involved in trying to cope with the number of members of the Spanish press who were likely to come over, and the numbers of VIPs who would want to attend the game. Of course, we were also conscious of the possibility of making substantially more money by going to Lansdowne Road.

After considering it overnight, I made the decision that the match should go on in Lansdowne Road, particularly in view of the fact that the FAI had got a good deal from the IRFU and were prepared to row in to help us run the game. We then announced the change and had to take numerous phone calls that afternoon from the media, asking us to explain why we had switched venues. We said that, due to the size of the game, our difficulties in trying to manage such a match in Tolka, and the fact that we hoped to make more money from the tie, we had no option but to transfer the game.

I spoke to Pat Fenlon about the change and, while he was extremely disappointed, in his usual professional way he accepted that it was in the interest of the club that it would be transferred. His subsequent TV and radio interviews did him great credit. He very clearly indicated that, from a football point of view he would have liked the match at Tolka but that he accepted that the overall interests of the supporters and the club probably meant that it had to be transferred. In this particular instance, Pat once again showed why he is so successful as a manager: he doesn't just have the necessary football skills, but he also has the ability to see the business side of things when necessary.

We then had all the difficulties of planning the game for more than double the attendance we would have expected in Tolka Park, as well as the question of deciding the price. We collectively decided that we would keep the price at €20 in order to indicate to our supporters that, while we needed – and wanted – to make money out of the tie, it wasn't all about that.

The decision to set the ticket price at €20 rather than €25 cost us more than €100,000, and in the ensuing weeks we got very little credit for our decision. Despite the fact that RTÉ that week had a programme that dealt with the high price of tickets at sporting events, nobody seemed to remember the gesture we had made. On the other hand, it was one of the few sporting occasions that I remember in Ireland where there were absolutely no negatives coming across from the media, the public or anybody else. Everybody seemed to be positive about the tie and about our handling of the event.

The night in Lansdowne Road was perhaps the greatest the club has ever seen. The players performed brilliantly on the pitch and the arrangements went exceptionally well. We decided to invite the Shelbourne players who had beaten Belenenses on a memorable night in 1962 to be guests at the match. It was great to meet them again.

There was a significant step up in protocol, administration and attention to detail that had to be addressed in running a match like that one. We had a corporate dinner before the match for two hundred people, a reception after the match for invited guests, and a separate reception for the players, all three in Lansdowne Road.

On the day of the match, there is always a formal meeting with the UEFA official during which he goes through every detail of the arrangements for the match. This person is UEFA's observer at the match, and he must give a written report to UEFA on the handling of the event by the home club. There is also a referee's representative from UEFA observing the referee's performance. All of these people have to be collected from the airport and looked after during their visit. I should point out: looked after but not bribed, as is reported to have happened in some eastern European countries!

The night before all European Cup matches, there is a dinner for the visiting club directors. We entertained the directors of Deportivo La Coruña in the Guinness Storehouse. Paul Carty of the Storehouse, and Diageo, were extremely generous and did a good deal for us. The Spaniards were suitably impressed, as is usually the case with people who visit Guinness.

On the night of the match, the Taoiseach, Bertie Ahern, attended, having come back from his holidays in Kerry for the match – something we very much appreciated. The atmosphere was electric; the support of the twenty-four thousand people in Lansdowne gave the players a great boost.

Unfortunately, we were not able to use the terraces at the two ends of the ground for spectators due to UEFA rules that, for these matches, all spectators must be seated. Despite looking for a derogation on two occasions, including using the fact that the Taoiseach was attending the match, UEFA refused to let us use the terracing behind the goals. Rather than have the ends look bare, however, we placed all our supporters' flags in that area and gave the impression that the area was occupied.

Despite the fact that their club had been so successful in Europe, the Deportivo directors were very complimentary to us, encouraging our efforts to achieve similar success in Europe. They indicated at the dinner that they had been in a similar position to us ten years previously but that they had now played in the Champions League in each of the previous five years.

We were soon made aware of the size of the club we were playing when we discovered that they had a €30 million wage bill and that their annual running costs were €80 million! All this, while operating in an area of only a quarter of a million people, as against the million-strong population of Dublin.

One thing that the Lansdowne Road experience proved was that the Wimbledon idea could have worked and that a team playing in European competition, whether in the Champions League or in a newly formed European league, would have the support of around 30,000 people for each match. We could have sold another 15,000 to 20,000 tickets for the Deportivo match.

The tie captivated the public imagination, and clubs from all over Ireland wished us well. Supporters from all over the country travelled to the match, and generally there was a great air of excitement. People who knew nothing about football seemed to have captured the mood of the game. Indeed, the viewing figures for TV3's coverage of Manchester United in the Champions

League on the same night, was 110,000 less than for RTÉ's broadcast of our match. Nobody would have believed that Shelbourne could 'outperform' Manchester United in this way or that people would pay €200 on the black market, as they did, to see Shelbourne play. We had definitely arrived!

While the team performed brilliantly on the night and would not have been flattered by a win, a nil-nil draw was a magnificent result with which everybody was happy – except the players, who seemed to feel that they might have edged it. The fact that the visitors didn't get an away goal was also a big boost for us when it came to the return leg.

The media coverage was exceptionally good for the club over this period of time, but some of the speculation about the amount of money that Shelbourne was going to make from it – around €1 million, according to one report – was way off the mark. What people seemed not to realise was that we had invested heavily over three years in developing a full-time squad in order to get to this position – and had accumulated substantial debts in the process.

When we travelled to Spain for the return leg, we filled three planes, and many others travelled overland, and from holiday resorts in Spain. As a result, on the night we had about a thousand supporters at the match.

The whole set-up in Deportivo was in another league compared to ours. The stadium itself, while it held only thirty-five thousand supporters, was compact and tiered. It also had a magnificent location on the seafront at the end of a beautiful promenade.

On the Friday, I flew out with the players, and that night I wandered across to the ground to see what it was like. To my surprise, I met two of the directors of the club outside the ground, and with many gestures managed to ask if I could see the stadium. They brought me in and showed me around. A match was about to start, but I decided not to wait, as I felt that my presence at the game might be seen as spying. The directors indicated it was their B team playing and dismissed it as a non-match, but later, when I got back to the hotel, the game was on the television, and eight or nine of their first team were on the pitch!

Our players were very confident that they would give a good display of themselves and get a result. Pat Fenlon's preparation for the match was first-class in every way: there had been great attention to detail in relation to food, medical care and physiotherapy. Everything was done to perfection, with nothing being left to chance, even down to bringing tins of baked beans, in case the hotel didn't have any!

The players had a free day on the Friday we arrived, apart from a swim in the sea outside the hotel. On Saturday, they trained twice, and Gary Browne and I travelled out with them to the evening training session to have a look at Deportivo's facilities. It was about half an hour from their main ground, and we were extremely impressed with the size of the ground and the range of the amenities provided.

In walking around the town, it was clear that our supporters were getting more and more confident – not over-confident, I hoped – that we could get a result and break through into the Champions League group play-offs.

The mission we were on was the equivalent of the one undertaken by the United States in 1950, when they beat England 1–0 in the World Cup, at a time when they were seen as a non-soccer country. If we were to beat Deportivo, it would create the same vibrations around Europe and would come as the same kind of surprise as the United States' victory.

It was quietly pointed out to the players that they were only ninety minutes from immortality and that they would be remembered forever if they made this breakthrough. Very often in life, you get very close to achieving your major objective and, having failed, weeks, months or years later, as you look back, you realise exactly how close you were, and that the objective was in fact achievable. Ireland's performance in Saipan was probably an example of this lack of awareness. In hindsight, it is clear that, on the day that Spain beat us with ten men, we didn't realise how close we were to getting to the final of the World Cup.

I believed that Deportivo were going through a difficult

period, with financial and team problems, and were there to be taken. Subsequently, their poor performance in Europe seemed to prove the point.

The build-up to the match was tremendous: the preparations with the players, Pat Fenlon's attention to detail and to keeping them motivated, fit and occupied so that boredom wouldn't be a problem in La Coruña from Friday to Tuesday. Excitement was added by the fans arriving on the day of the match walking the prom and walking to the ground from the hotel in the blazing sunshine at eight in the evening for the nine o'clock kick-off.

The match itself was a roller-coaster ride – in the first half very good for us, and in the second half not so good. For fifty minutes we performed very well but, just as Deportivo were becoming frustrated, we made a mistake and were severely punished. I was sitting beside the president of Deportivo and, at half-time, he was very worried. Elimination for them would have been a financial disaster. The match, unfortunately, turned out to be a disappointment for us, though. We were beaten 3–0, a score we really didn't deserve, having performed so brilliantly in the first half and, in addition, having had Pat Fenlon and Alan Moore sent off.

I suppose the most satisfying sight was seeing the Shelbourne supporters still applauding fifteen minutes after the game had finished, when the team came back out on the pitch. Seeing all the young people and children in their red-and-white gear for the match, living the experience of a lifetime, was a tremendous experience.

There is also the memory of the excitement of my grandson, Josh, coming to the match in his new suit – dark, with a dark shirt and blue tie – which he insisted on bringing to Spain to wear for the match. He insists on wearing this outfit on all special occasions and seems to become quite a young gentleman when he has it on! He enjoyed the formalities – shaking hands and standing by my side to greet people. He was interviewed by Sky News afterwards and, to my amazement, responded to all the questions asked by the reporter. A friend of mine in England saw the interview on TV and sent me a text message to say that

Josh had made more sense than the chairman!

Despite the defeat, the great adventure continued as we headed for the UEFA draw – which gave us another game in Europe, against Lille of France. Our dealings with Lille turned into a nightmare, with the relationship between the officers of the two clubs being anything but friendly. From the beginning, we understood that the match in Dublin would be televised by French TV; as a result, we arranged to play at 5.30 PM. For various reasons, we switched the match to Lansdowne Road – a decision that became more and more controversial as the day of the game drew nearer.

UEFA had decided that Tolka Park, with its limitations, was not suitable for European football, beyond the preliminary rounds. The main reason for switching was that the lights in Tolka Park were classified as unsuitable, following the UEFA observer's report on the Hajduk Split game. We also wanted to encourage the supporters who had come to see Deportivo to stay with us in Europe by attending again.

Unfortunately, the TV deal fell through, and when we suggested changing the starting time of the match back to 7.45 PM, Lille refused to agree to the change. Although the mother and father of all battles then took place between Ollie Byrne and his counterpart in the French club, Lille refused to budge. Eventually, after the involvement of UEFA and our TV agents in France, Lille agreed to a 7 PM kick-off. This, while an improvement, lost us a significant number of supporters. As it turned out, the weather was terrible for the match: the rain poured down from about 4 PM, and there was a lot of thunder during the match. The one good thing to come out of the starting-time row was that their club president landed in his personal jet in Dublin at 6 PM and, due to heavy traffic, arrived at the ground twenty minutes after the start. I got great pleasure in telling them that, if they had agreed to the 7.45 PM kick-off time, he would have made it to the ground for the beginning of the match!

Our performance in the first half was poor, and at half-time we were 2–0 down. Pat Fenlon watched the match from the stand, having been banned for two games after being sent off in Spain. The second half was better for us, though, and we scored two late goals, to finish 2–2. It was still all to play for in Lille!

Our trip to Lille, for some reason, was something of a disappointment, not only from the football point of view but also as an experience. The city itself didn't have the same atmosphere as previous places we had travelled to, possibly because there was no organised club trip for supporters. On the field, Lille turned out to be everything I feared they might – skilful and fast, a better side than Deportivo. Our players did extremely well to hold them to a 2–0 defeat.

The president of the club was an interesting character. He was a movie mogul and told me that he saw the club as similar to the film industry, with the manager being the director, the coach as the producer, and some of the players the prima donnas! His brother owns Lyons, who were the French league champions in 2005. The two brothers owned the champions and runners-up in the French league in 2005!

The summer of 2004 was magic – a magnificent adventure in Europe for Shelbourne supporters, while at home most other clubs seemed to be in disarray both financially and on the pitch. Football supporters began talking in terms of it being a disaster that Shelbourne were so far ahead of the rest, arguing that this is not good for either football in Ireland or the Eircom League.

It was clear from talking to various media people that the expectation was that we would maintain this momentum, but I was not convinced that we had the necessary resources. I believe that it is possible, in any organisation, to slip quickly back down the success ladder. Unless there is a strong input of finance and greater concentration on our administrative skills, we will not be able to perform at the level that is expected of us – that is, competing with similar clubs in Europe. Like many organisations, on occasion our reputation exceeds our performance.

*

We at Shelbourne Football Club are facing into a new era, which will hopefully see the future of the club being secured. With costs of more than €2 million a year to run the club, and debts that we have accumulated through playing full-time football, it is essential that we reduce our costs. The only way of doing this is to sell Tolka Park. Otherwise, it will mean reverting to part-time football and accepting that there are limits to what the Eircom League can deliver. In other countries, where teams have done well in Europe, they have been heavily subsidised by either their football associations or their government. Without that kind of assistance, or significant corporate sponsorship, it will not be possible to achieve what we believe is possible for us in terms of European football. Shelbourne's run in the competition in 2004 has proved that the dream of Champions League football is achievable.

Over the last fifteen years or so, Shelbourne has been one of the most successful clubs in the Eircom League; many would say, the most successful. We have played in European competitions every year except one over this period. On a number of occasions during this time, we have come close to getting past the first rounds but have only done so twice. Now, however, with the benefit of a full-time squad to draw on, we are better placed than ever to be successful in Europe.

In the past, winning the league or the Cup was the key objective of clubs here, but the clubs who are making big investments in full-time football are now looking to progress successfully to the group stages of the Champions League. Qualification for Europe is essential but of itself is not enough.

Shelbourne believe that it is a very realistic ambition for an Irish club to qualify for the group stages of the Champions League in the next five years, provided that there is a robust business plan to finance the increased cost involved. We believe that Shelbourne, of all the clubs in the league, is the one that is best positioned to achieve this breakthrough.

In line with the strategy of the successful clubs in small countries like our own, Shelbourne has developed a thriving underage football section, comprising seventeen teams. These include some of the best young soccer talent in the country. An emphasis on youth football seems to us to be a prerequisite to success in Europe, and Shelbourne has moved to put that important foundation stone in place.

The embracing of full-time professionalism by Shelbourne comes about as a result of the club trying to put into practice in Ireland the lessons it has learned from comparable European role models. Major difficulties remain, however. Unless a club achieves success in the next few years, the whole question of full-time football in the country will have to be reviewed, with negative results for football in Ireland in the longer term. At the moment, a number of clubs are creating financial difficulties for themselves by trying to compete with the big clubs.

The 2005 season started badly for us, with our players sustaining injuries and the team losing a number of league games that we were expected to win. Far from being way ahead of the chasing pack, we failed to defend our position as league champions successfully. I was pleased, however, that Damien Richardson, for whom I have great respect, was successful, given the near-misses he has had over the years.

The year 2006 will be a key one for Shelbourne on and off the pitch. We must restore our position as Eircom League champions in order to get to where we need to be – in the Champions League. On the business side, our discussions on ground-sharing with Bohemians will dominate. Reaching an agreement will require great cooperation and trust on both sides. The involvement of the FAI will be a great help in our efforts to reach an agreement.

5

# The Final Chapter?

When I retired from the Labour Court in 2003, I expected to be heading off into the sunset for a nice, easy retirement. Within a very short time, however, I was invited back by Kevin Duffy, the chairman of the court, to act as deputy chairman for a few months while the post was advertised and filled. I thoroughly enjoyed my few months back in the court, watching Kevin take on all the responsibilities and pressures of running the place.

Since then, I have worked as hard as I have ever worked in my life, having taken over as chairman of the government's Decentralisation Implementation Group and also as chairman of the St. Michael's Regeneration Board. I have also acted in a consultancy capacity to a large number of companies on a wide range of issues. I now find that I am working five days a week – and longer days than I have worked for many years. I am not complaining, however: I love the work and the variety, and in particular I love the challenge.

In looking back over my fifty years working in the public and private sectors, I am conscious that I have been lucky enough to have held three of the most prestigious, challenging and interesting posts in the country. During this period, I have had the privilege of working with people of the highest integrity and standards. I have also, unfortunately, had the misfortune of coming across some people for whom I would have little regard – in some cases, arrogant opportunists riding on the backs of others.

Many changes have taken place both in society and in business over the last fifty years. The changes in both areas have had major implications for all of us, whether we are operating in the business world or as members of a rapidly changing society, just trying to survive in a world that seems to change on a daily basis.

The level and pace of change that has taken place is phenomenal, and there is no reason to believe that the changes that lie ahead will not be even more dramatic. The requirement in management for people with the ability to bring about change is a priority, and it will be the key to success well into the future.

During my management career, I found managing change to be one of the most challenging, exciting and stimulating aspects of my work, particularly when managing change in a successful company. When there is a crisis in an organisation, it is clear to everyone that there is a problem, and usually employees are more inclined to accept change in order to ensure the survival of the organisation than they would otherwise be. The bigger challenge, however, is to try to bring about the required changes in a successful organisation: real skill and leadership are essential to achieve this.

Companies cannot avoid change, but they can influence the effect it has on their organisation. Frequently, however, companies avoid making the necessary strategic decisions because top management takes the soft option and avoids biting the bullet when radical action is required. Thus, too frequently, the seeds of failure are sown in the complacency of success. It has always been my view that companies, and indeed countries, are at their most vulnerable when they are at their strongest financially. It is then that they avoid taking the necessary remedial action.

Managing change is about leadership. The days of blind acceptance of the instructions of those in positions of authority have long gone. Indeed, this approach has in the past had devastating consequences for many people in our society. This is clear from the revelations of the tribunals into child abuse,

222

where religious and state leaders who were given blind obedience by the public failed in their responsibilities towards the innocent.

In organisations today, people have to be led: they will not follow blindly. Companies that continue to be over-managed and under-led struggle and will, in the long term, fail. Nonetheless, leaders also have to be accepted. Chairmen, chief executives and directors of organisations can be appointed, but leaders only become leaders when those who are to be led accept them.

People in all walks of life look to their leaders for vision, courage, honesty, integrity and trust. Unfortunately, many, whether in business, politics or religion, are experiencing severe shortfalls in many of these attributes and as a consequence are becoming disillusioned with their role.

Over the years, I have been asked on many occasions and by many people what were the key requirements for getting to the top of an organisation. In responding to this question, I have always indicated that, in addition to having ability, you need a large slice of luck and to be in the right place at the right time.

Speaking of my own career, it was ironic that the attributes that had got me into so much trouble throughout my early working life were subsequently viewed by the company as being exactly what it required. Many people find themselves in similar positions, possessing skills that their companies do not want at a particular time or, worse still, that their managers fail to appreciate. In such circumstances, individuals should look elsewhere and 'sell' their skills to someone who wants and will appreciate these skills. If they choose to stay in organisations where they are not valued, they should stop moaning, get on with life and become single-handicap golfers, only looking to the company to pay their mortgages.

Everyone must manage their own career: while companies can put in place training programmes and succession plans, it is the responsibility of all of us to make personal assessments of our situation on a regular basis. Professional football taught me that the secret of success in managing my career was to be on the lookout for the next club. Similarly, in a work situation, it is important to be looking around to see where the next promotion or the next job might be within the organisation, or even outside of it.

Another requirement for success is the ability to keep your eyes and ears open. Many people in organisations fail to observe what is happening around them. Successful people are usually very politically aware: they seem to anticipate what is likely to happen and to be able to look around corners, following company politics carefully.

Some managers believe that merely doing a good job is sufficient for further success. It is not. Doing the job you are paid for is a given; it is the extra contribution that you bring to the job that makes the difference and singles out an individual for promotion. Successful managers will usually have their particular areas of responsibility ticking over smoothly, requiring very little attention and have the bulk of their time given over to the more visionary and creative aspects of the job, while all the time preparing for the next challenge.

In many organisations, people are promoted well beyond their level of competence. The more clever of these, however, make sure that this fact is never discovered! They quietly do their job and never create hassle. Nonetheless, the fact that somebody in a particular area seems to be operating without any problems does not necessarily mean that they are doing a good job: it can also mean that they are ignoring or burying problems. This is usually the case when dealing with what I call a corporate marionette. The corporate marionette is somebody who performs only when someone above them is around. They will become animated and extremely active when anybody who can affect the progress of their career in a positive way is in the vicinity. Once the person to be impressed goes out of range, the individual relaxes again and gives little attention to the individuals they are working with, seeing them as being of no great value to them.

Some individuals have made personal career management an art and have used it to their own rather than the organisation's benefit. They are past masters at managing their careers while contributing very little to the success of the organisation.

'Career managers' often have a number of similar traits across companies. They make sure that they are never associated with any problem which could be damaging to their career. Implementation is something they avoid like the plague, there are no brownie points for implementing change, and attempting to do so can carry great risks. They usually move quite quickly through the organisation – sometimes sideways for a spell rather than upwards – but they never stay too long in one place because they might have to deliver.

These people are also very keen on 'observable movement': they are always buzzing around – in early, staying late, if the boss is there, and appearing to be doing something important. These people's contribution or achievements can in effect be negligible, however.

Many careerists are soft-option people: they go for the quick fix and avoid confrontation. Confrontation attracts attention and can damage your image and career, whereas appeasement is less career-threatening. These people will always 'pay the ransom', ignoring the long-term consequences for the company.

Some companies have people in senior management positions who no longer meet the requirements of the organisation. In many instances, however, the people who should tackle these problems choose to ignore them and leave individuals in key parts of the organisation, even though they know they are not performing. This can be particularly damaging at senior-executive or board level. The failure to tackle the problem can arise for a number of reasons: the person responsible may not have the managerial skills or courage to deal with the problem, or he or she may hope to be moving on and leaving the problem to somebody else. More often, no action is taken because of what I call the 'golf' or 'social' syndrome.

The golf syndrome is when people at a high level in an organisation play a foursome of golf every weekend. In this situation, it may be very difficult to tackle a problem within this group: 'What will happen the foursome? We won't be able to play together again: the atmosphere will be terrible.'

The social syndrome is even worse. This is when people at a particular level socialise with each other, visiting each other's houses on a regular basis. Now, suddenly, one of them has to deal with the inadequacy of a colleague who is part of the social forum. Facing up to having to move that person, with all of the consequences that will ensue – families not talking, bitterness creeping in – is often too much for them. Once again, the person who should make the decision puts off doing so in the hope that something will happen in the meantime – that the particular person might decide to retire early, for instance.

One of the things I discovered over the course of my career is that, as a junior or middle manager, you are expected by your superior to know everything about the organisation. Invariably, when the superior is in trouble with the people above them, they will come to you and expect you to dig out the information that is required. The remarkable thing is that, the further you go up the organisation, the less you have to know, because all around you are people who know everything.

As a junior in the Traffic Department, working with Harry Hannon – one of the best developers of managers and one of the best motivators I have ever met – I was expected to know all about marketing, accounting, sales and everything else to do with the business, even those areas in which I had no active role. Harry would ring up at any time of the day and ask questions, with the result that I and my colleagues were always on our toes, studying what was happening in the broader organisation, with a view to having the information if he rang. I learnt to use all the knowledge and skills that I had developed to benefit the organisation.

A leader can never show indecision or uncertainty. This has a disastrous effect within the top team and on the organisation. While the leader may not have all the answers, he or she must always be seen to have the vision, courage and ability to lead the organisation to the 'promised land'.

The pressure on business leaders and people in the early

stages of a career – working long hours and experiencing tremendous stress – often takes its toll on home life and relationships. Sometimes this price is too high.

Life for young people today is very different from how it was in my time. While they have more career opportunities, they must survive in a more competitive world. When we were growing up, we had security – very few rights, but security. As the author Charles Handy has written, we have swapped security for choice. The security we fell back on is gone: family life is not as secure as it was, and the institutions that formed our lives and gave us direction have, mostly, been discredited. Many young people make key career decisions based on family tradition, or Leaving Certificate marks, and subsequently find themselves following a career they hate.

I would say to young people starting off in their careers that they must decide whether they want to be opportunists or careerists or someone who makes a genuine contribution. It is essential that young people make sure that they fulfil their potential: that is all anyone can expect. Many people coast through life thinking they are conning everyone, but in fact it is only themselves they are conning by not fulfilling their potential. Decide what you want and go for it but, most of all, make a difference.

People must speak their mind and stand up for what they believe in. Too many nowadays play the game or join the club, and fail to ask why or to say 'stop'. It is unfortunate that the image of business, and indeed society, today has been tarnished to the extent that young people have no confidence in institutions. One young man in the Institute of Technology in Waterford some years ago told me that 'To do well in business one has to be devious, cunning and dishonest.' This is a sad reflection on our society today.

Ireland has been tremendously successful over the last twenty years, moving from a situation where the World Bank was threatening to move in, unemployment stood at 18 percent and inflation was above 20 percent. There was a general air of doom and gloom around, and emigration was the scourge of the day.

Today, not only are we seeking workers from other countries to supplement our workforce, but we also have an economy that is the envy of Europe and are held up as an example for other small countries. Our success has been proclaimed all over the world, and we have become major players on the global scene.

While the success we have enjoyed economically over the last decade has resulted in major benefits, it has been achieved at a price. No longer are we the caring nation that we once were: people now strive to be the best and have the most. With materialism rampant, instant gratification is the order of the day. Our national financial performance has enabled us to deal with various problems that have developed in our society by throwing money at them. Bad behaviour is rewarded in all walks of life, and standards that would not have been acceptable to previous generations have now become the norm. Indeed, in some ways the Ireland of today resembles the USA of twenty years ago – something we used to look at aghast on our television screens.

Our new-found wealth has failed to resolve many of the problems that existed before we started on our successful run, particularly in the health and education sectors. We still have a situation where the health service, particularly Accident and Emergency Departments, is totally unacceptable, with people, many of them elderly, on trolleys while they wait for a bed. We have schools that are unfit for children to attend. We have carers working twenty-four hours a day looking after family members and not getting respite because the necessary financial provision has not been made to enable them to get a break.

It is nearly impossible for young people to get the money together to take the first step on the property ladder, and we have people travelling three and four hours a day to get to and from their place of employment. We have parents afraid for the safety of their children going out at night because of the violence on our streets. We have tribunals costing millions, sitting for years, to prove what most people knew already, and projected to continue for many more years, at a cost of millions more. All we seem to be concerned about is the fact that the economy is doing well!

The measure of a caring society is how it deals with the weakest in the community, but unfortunately, those who are not capable of causing disruption or influencing elections are less likely to be heard, whereas those who shout loudest are listened to. As we move into a multicultural society, we must take time to decide what kind of society we want, what kind of priorities we want to set, and what kind of issues we want to tackle in order to improve the quality of life for all our people.

After fifty years working, what does the future hold for me? A very good friend of mine, John Hudson, often joked about himself that 'My future is behind me.' I thought my future was behind me when I left the Labour Court, but that does not seem to have been the case: happily, I continue to make a contribution wherever and whenever I can.

My work as chairman of the Fatima Regeneration Project, which is responsible for rebuilding Fatima Mansions, gives me great satisfaction, particularly when I see the first houses being occupied. The additional role I took on last year of chairing the St Michael's Regeneration Board will ensure that I am kept busy!

This book will, I hope, give my two grandsons some idea of what their grandfather's life was like. In conclusion, I would like to thank the many people who have helped me during my fifty-plus working years in the Brewery, in the Labour Court and in my football career. I would like this book to stand as a tribute to all of them.